collector's guide to
TOASTERS
& ACCESSORIES

identification & values

Helen Greguire

COLLECTOR BOOKS
A Division of Schroeder Publishing Co., Inc.

The current values in this book should be used only as a guide. They are not intended to set prices, which vary from one section of the country to another. Auction prices as well as dealer prices vary greatly and are affected by condition as well as demand. Neither the Author nor the Publisher assumes responsibility for any losses that might be incurred as a result of consulting this guide.

Searching for a Publisher?

We are always looking for knowledgeable people considered to be experts within their fields. If you feel that there is a real need for a book on your collectible subject and have a large comprehensive collection, contact Collector Books.

On the Cover:

Top Right: *Excelsior Twin Reversible Toaster $675.00.*
Center: *Toastrite "Blue Willow" Pattern Toaster $3,500.00.*
Bottom: *Star-Rite Automatic Toaster $145.00.*

Cover design: Beth Summers
Book design: Sherry Kraus
Photography: Frederick Greguire III

Additional copies of this book may be ordered from:

COLLECTOR BOOKS
P.O. Box 3009
Paducah, Kentucky 42002–3009

or

Helen Greguire
103 Trimmer Road
Hilton, New York 14468

@ $19.95. Add $2.00 for postage and handling.

Contents

Acknowledgments

Putting together a book requires the knowledge and collective efforts of many people and collectors. I am fortunate to have the best of both. Special appreciation goes out to my family.

To my husband Fred, thanks for taking me all over the country to places I didn't even know existed in search of toasters.

To my son Fred Greguire III who did all of the photography for the book, and the patience he acquired in typing my handwritten material, and to his wife Valerie.

To my daughter and son-in-law, MaryLou and Paul Prince for the loan of their toasters and accessories. And to my granddaughter Paula, and great-grandson John Erick.

My sincere thanks to all who have helped me find toasters, loaned me their choice toasters from their collections, copied and sent literature. Thank you for the help in making this book a reality: Nancy Higginson, Charly Grossman, Terry and Cathy Seacrist, Richard and Geraldine Smiszek, Brenda Hutto, Rose Schleede, Lillian Cole, Patricia McKaughn, Muriel and Lewis DeFrank.

To Howard Hazelcorn, one of the first to author a book on toasters, *Hazelcorn's Price Guide to Old Electric Toasters*, which is now updated with latest prices and has more toasters added. Because of the knowledgeable research concerning companies and toasters, I feel this book would be a good companion book to mine. It may be ordered from Howard and Jane Hazelcorn, 6731 Ashley Court, Sarasota, Florida 34241. The price is $19.95 postage paid.

Last but not least, my sincere thanks to Jim Hyde, a true collector whose enthusiasm just seems to bubble over when he finds or talks about toasters. Here is a sample of one of our "typical" conversations. My phone rings. "It's Jim, I've found some toasters and thought maybe you'd like to see them and also photograph them for your book." I reply, "Oh, yes, I'll see you in 15 minutes." It's like Christmas and waiting for Santa to come with all his packages. When he opens them, it's "Oh!!! Gee! Gosh, that's a great one." Wow. Then he tells me the stories of how he got them and how many miles he traveled. I believe another special person should also be mentioned, and this is Jim's wife Katie for assisting Jim on his adventures. Her stories are great. She told me how one time it was pouring down rain, she was soaked to the skin, her sneakers were soaking wet, and Jim decided she should have some rain gear to protect her and, of course, the toasters. Besides Katie's being Jim's wife, she is also his runner and carrier. This means Katie can carry at least four toasters, and Jim is always careful to make sure Katie keeps those toasters dry. Finally the hunt is over for the day, Jim having no trouble falling asleep in the van, and Katie trying to figure out how to dry her clothes and sneaks. Did I mention he already had rain gear before it started to pour?

Now I ask you, wouldn't this world be a dull place to live if we could not encounter some of these delightful collecting experiences?

A Golden Toast to You All,
Helen Greguire

Why Collect Toasters and Accessories

It is important to choose a collectible that people have a general familiarity with as well as being desirable, affordable, and even usable. Toasters and accessories are *all* of that.

Toasters and accessories are also cross collectibles because they fit into the kitchen collectible category as well, and as you probably are aware, kitchen collectibles are very popular today.

Toasters are fascinating and unique works of art. I, along with many others, am intrigued by their blend of electrical, mechanical, and aesthetic design. Accessories that are available for some of the toasters make collecting the whole set very challenging. Some of these items may include matching coffee pots, urns, sugars, creamers, sandwich toasters, toast racks, and trays.

I truly enjoy collecting toasters and their accessories, which has led me to share with all of you my collection as well as the knowledge I have gained over the years.

A number of books have been done on researching the companies, patents, dates, and histories but the purpose of this book is to show you what is available in toasters and accessories. I'm sure there are a number of you out there who will say, "I have a toaster that is not in the book." No matter how large a book, there is no way to include every toaster.

I have made an effort to preserve part of our American heritage in photographs and literature for future generations who might have never known the uses for these things. In reading this book I hope you better understand the reasons I see value in collecting toasters and accessories.

About the Author

Writing is nothing new for Helen Greguire. Her first published book on carnival glass, titled *Carnival in Lights* is still much in demand.

By the late 1980s, Helen's collection of granite ware had grown to such an extent, and her expertise on the subject had become so widely known that she decided to share some of the knowledge with others in two volumes of the *Collector's Encyclopedia of Granite Ware*.

The demand for Helen Greguire as a national speaker is ever increasing. When not traveling around the country buying, selling, or lecturing, Helen enjoys being at her beautiful country home in Hilton, N.Y. She also spends much of her time helping other collectors to more fully enjoy their hobbies.

Ever since I can remember, my mom and dad have been involved with one form of antiques or another, especially my mom, Helen Greguire.

As I was growing up, I vividly remember my parents' awesome Carnival Glass collection which was eventually overrun by Mom's extensive collection of Granite Ware. And just when I thought she was content, about 8 or 10 years ago, we started to see these toasters appear among the other antiques in her country kitchen. Then before you knew it, there were china cabinets full of these chrome "works of art," as she calls them.

And now Mom's collection has grown to well over 500 toasters. And she is constantly having my father drive her all over the countryside to find "just one more."

Over the period of time that she has been collecting, her knowledge of the subject has greatly expanded. I truly believe that her main goal with this book is to reach out to friends and fellow collectors to share the fun, excitement, and love of collecting toasters, as she has in her other books on Granite Ware and Carnival Glass.

Fred Greguire III

Toaster Collectors Newsletter & Assoc.

For free information send SASE to:
A Toast To You/ Upper Crust • P. O. Box 529 • Teme, CA 92590 • (909)-699-8456

If you are seeking information or have questions for the author, please send SASE to:
Helen Greguire — Toasters • 103 Trimmer Road • Hilton, NY 14468 • (716)-392-2704

"Hotwire" — The Toaster Museum Foundation
P.O. Box 11886 • Portland, OR 97211-0886 • 503-287-2115 • Editor: Eric Norcross

In Search of the National Toaster Society

At the time of the writing of this book, I am avidly seeking others who would be interested in starting a National Toaster Society.

As a member of other national organizations, I feel such groups stir excitement in a particular area of collecting, in this case toasters and accessories. I would eventually like to see a nationwide membership as well as a national convention where we would gather to show our finds and share our common interest of collecting toasters and accessories.

Anyone who would be interested in helping form this organization, I would be happy to hear from you, and would welcome any suggestions you might have on how to help form it. Please feel free to contact me at (716)-392-2704.

Sincerely,
Helen Greguire

Introduction

Although non-electric toasters did exist before the early 1900s, the electric toaster evolved from Albert Marsh's invention of "the nickel-chromium alloy with contents being very low in electrical conductivity, very infusible, non-oxidizable to a very high degree, tough and sufficiently ductile to permit drawing or shaping it into a wire for use as an electrical resistance element," the alloy that would be used for heating elements in early electric toasters.

Marsh was granted his patent on Tuesday, February 6, 1906. The Haskins Manufacturing Co. then formed to develop uses and markets for Marsh's invention. In the late 1909 consumer market the table cooker called the "Toaststove" was invented. And now a whole new electrical era had begun. However, there was one major problem: the power companies. Electricity was very expensive and limited in supply. Not until 1912 with the expansion of alternating current, did electricity become more efficient and economical than the existing direct current produced by the reactionary Edison empire. And with this development came the rush to the market place with new and improved products, including heating appliances and toasters. Toasters were relative late-comers to this new market.

As you will see, toasters were crafted in numerous "Works of Art." Toasters with their accessories were actually the delightful center of attention over the years, whether used at morning, noon, or night.

Toasters and their accessories have taken on a new perspective today. Not only are they usable, with care and attention to what type of electrical outlet should be used, they are also cherished by numerous collectors today for their beauty as well as their ingenious electrical mechanics.

Pricing Information

What I have tried to achieve in this price guide is an approximate suggested price for each item, even though different areas of the country and abroad can demand a higher or lower price.

Many factors help to determine the price, including condition, rarity, color, shape, size, age, popularity, manufacturer, production location, original accessories, and cross collectibility. All these factors will help to determine a premium price.

Condition is of prime importance when setting up a price guide. The prices given in this book are for toasters in good working order, good finish to the metal, no chips or cracks in the handles, knobs, feet, or base, and also matching cord and plug unless otherwise stated.

Another point of interest is some later model toasters bring a higher premium than some earlier models, because some toasters are more desirable because of their design. Example: some Art Deco style toasters demand a higher value because of their unique aesthetic design compared to some of the more common earlier models.

Another factor that can make a toaster demand a higher price is a unique design in the electrical and/or mechanical works. An example of this is the Toast-A-Lator toaster, which has the bread move through the toaster on a chain style conveyor system. This is the only toaster that I know of that moves the toast while toasting.

Toasters that have no heat control devices and are totally manually will usually demand less than the automatics.

The Blue and Pink Willow pattern toasters are a prime example of a toaster fitting into a number of categories. For instance these toasters are rare, unique in color and shape, because of their age, and are popular as cross collectibles (also would be sought after by collectors of the Blue Willow pattern).

The Porcelier is a toaster with matching Procelier accessories. The toaster as well as its accessories, (coffee pot and urn, sugar, creamer, sandwich toaster, and waffle iron), are all decorated with a basketweave type pattern that has floral decoration.

The shape of a toaster can also make it more desirable and valuable. An example of this would be the Heart-Shaped toaster.

In summary, my personal opinion is that toasters and accessories are only worth what you or anyone else is willing to pay for them. A price guide is meant to be just that, a "guide." In an effort to bring to you the most accurate price for an item, I have compiled price lists from all over the country, as well as current auction prices, antique show prices, dealer prices, and private sales. My main purpose in trying to reach an appropriate figure is not to outprice toasters and accessories for collectors but on the other hand, I want to be realistic about an actual "going" price. If a collector after reading this guide were to see a toaster or accessory for sale at a higher price than what was mentioned, he or she might have passed it up because of the guide's unrealistic low price.

Prices in this guide are based on toasters in good working order and prime condition. I have to decline responsibility for any losses incurred from this guide.

TOASTERS

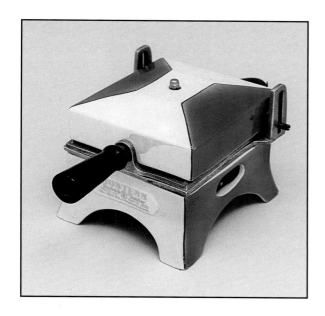

ALL RITE CO.
Hostess Single Sandwich, 1930s, 4¾" high by 5¼" wide and 4⅞" long, pearlized iridescent porcelain body with blue sections. I have seen other color variations in this sandwich toaster such as a green and light lavender. Molded nameplate reads: "Hostess Sandwich Toaster Volts 110 Watts 400. All Rite Co. Rushville Ind." $285.00.

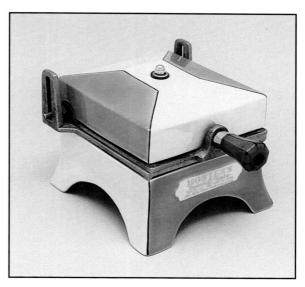

ALL RITE CO.
Hostess Single Sandwich, 1930s, 5¼" wide by 4⅞" long, pearlized iridescent porcelain body with green sections on cover. Molded front nameplate reads: "Hostess Sandwich Toaster Volts 110 Watts 400 All-Rite Co. Rushville Ind." The cover is supported by adjustable metal arms on the back of the toaster. $285.00.

ALL RITE CO.
Hostess Double Sandwich Toaster, 1930s, 5⅜" high by 6⅞" wide and 9⅜" long, decorated floral porcelain body. Molded nameplate reads: "Hostess Sandwich Toaster Volts 110 Watts 400 All-Rite Co. Rushville Ind. Note: The decorated hostess double sandwich toaster is extremely rare. $2,975.00.

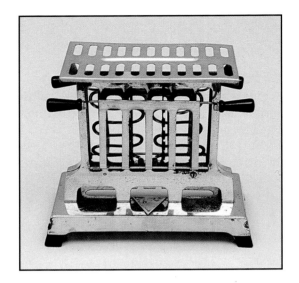

AMERICAN ELE TRICAL HEATER COMPANY

American Beauty, 1912 – 1915, 7⅜" high, nickel plated body with black wooden handles and feet, horizontal laced wire coil heating element, no heat control. Nameplate on front reads: "American Beauty Toaster." Bottom marked: "American Ele trical Heater Co. Detroit, USA LMP Patented September 10, 1912 March 10, 1914 March 9, 1915 Cat. No. 5825G." Note: the attached toast warming rack. Also note how the top rod on the door is designed outward so the wooden handles are not close to the body of the toaster. $100.00.

AMERICAN ELE TRICAL HEATER COMPANY

Rite-Heat Glower Toast Stove, 1920s, 3⅜" high by 5" long and 5" wide, nickel plated body, no heat control. Marked: "Rite-Heat Glower Toast Stove Cat. No. 3350G Volts 110-125 Watts 500 American Ele Trical Heater Company. Made in Detroit USA Patents Pending." $25.00.

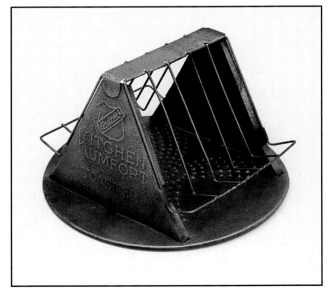

ANDROCK

Kitchen Kumfort Toaster, early 1900s, 5¼" high, stove top which is non-electric, pierced tin and wire. Marked on each end: "Androck Kitchen Kumfort Toaster. Patent apld. for U.S. & Canada." Note: The unique piercing on the bottom of the toaster. $55.00.

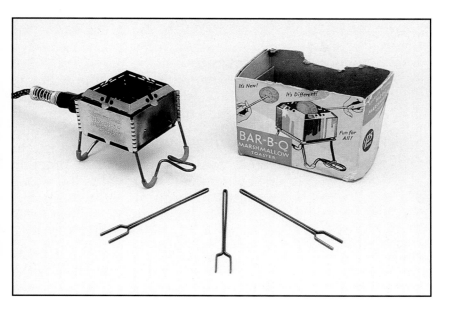

ANGELUS -CAMPFIRE BAR-B-Q MARSHMALLOW

with original box, cord and forks, late 1920s – early 1930s, 3¾" high with insert. Marked on the front and back sides: "Angelus-Campfire Bar-B-Q-Marshmallow Toaster. Patent Applied For. Volts 110 Watts 345." The metal forks are used to hold a single marshmallow down inside the toaster. $125.00 with original box, cord and forks.

ARMSTRONG

Perc-O-Toaster, 1920s, 13½" high, model PT. This one is shown with the black enamel base and the double plug. This double plug can also be used separately and can be plugged into a single outlet. $350.00 with black enamel base and double cord.

ARMSTRONG

Perc-O-Toaster, 1920s, 13½" high. Nameplate reads "Armstrong Perc-O-Toaster 440 Watts 575 Watts Model Pt. 110 Volts Pat. Applied For The Armstrong Elec. & Mfg. Corp Huntington, W.VA." The percolator is highly polished nickel and base is made in either nickel or china-white or black porcelain. An old ad states "Delicious Coffee and Toast Made With The New Armstrong Perc-O-Toaster (two appliances in one)...If you like waffles occasionally there is a waffle iron attachment that fits in the toaster compartment. Price $3.50 Extra, Price Only $11.85 Complete with cord and double plug." $275.00. *(See detail on next page.)*

ARMSTRONG

Perc-O-Toaster, I felt it important to show this unit taken apart. Note the unique plug design that shows the two flat prongs bulge out on the outer edge of the plug. In the ad it states "Perc-O-Toaster May Be Used Together or Separately, One Double Plug – One Outlet." This unit shows two special shaped plugs are used separately in two outlets. Consider yourself lucky if you find this unit with the cord and special plug. $275.00 with original plug.

ARMSTRONG

Table Stove, 1917 – 1922, 7⅛" high, white enamel. Pieces include broil pan with insert, toast rack, waffle iron, and egg poacher. Marked on the side: "Armstrong Table Stove The Armstrong Mfg. Co. W.VA. USA Volts 110 600 Watts Patented Oct. 9, 17 Apr. 23, 18 Dec. 12, 22 No. 813." $95.00 complete.

AUTO-TOASTMAKER

1930s, 8¼" high, nickel plated body, with wooden carrying handles, knobs, and feet. Nameplate reads "Auto-Toastmaker. Model No. 73. Pats Pend. Dark and Light Control Volts 110 Watts 600 Sears, Roebuck Co. Chicago Ill." Note: The beauty of the curved and embossed sides and door of this toaster. $250.00.

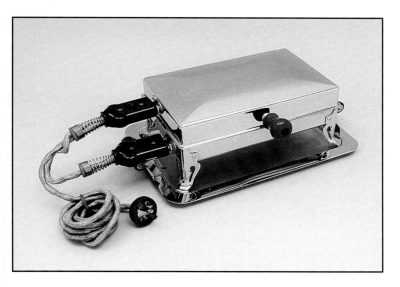

BEARDSLEY & WOLCOTT MFG. CO.
Torrid Flat, late 1920s, 4¼" high by 11¼" long and 7⅞" wide, nickel plated body with green wooden handles. Marked on the bottom: "Torrid The Beardsley & Wolcott Mfg. Co. Waterbury Conn Volts 110 Amps 5.5." No heat control. The double plugs are also marked "Torrid Hartford Conn. 600W 250V." Note: Toasters found with the original double plug demand a higher price because the double plugs are hard to find. $95.00 with double plug.

BEARDSLEY & WOLCOTT MFG. CO.
Torrid, 1920s, 6⅞" high, chrome plated body with black wooden knobs and fiber feet. Marked on bottom: "Torrid Beardsley & Wolcott Mfg. Co. Waterbury, Conn. Volts 110 Amps 4.8 Nov. 15, 1920 Feb. 15, 1927." Note: No heat controls. The baskets are controlled manually. Each one swings out separately and around on the two arms attached to the base of the toaster. $100.00.

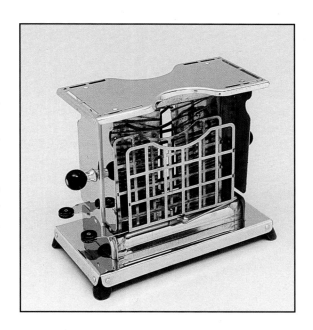

BEARDSLEY & WOLCOTT MFG. CO.
Torrid, 1930s, 7⅞" high, highly polished nickel body with black wooden carrying handles and fiber feet. Marked on the bottom: "Torrid. The Beardsley & Wolcott Mfg. Co. Waterbury Conn. Volts 110-Amps 6 Patents Appl'd. For." The bigger lever on the right front side of the toaster is pressed down, which shuts the inside slots that the bread rests on along the front door section. The smaller lever on the right side is then set for desired browning by raising it up or down according to the A thru F marks on the toaster. When toast is done, the inside slots flip down along with the door section on the front, and release the toast. This style toaster is sometimes referred to as a "dropper." $250.00.

BEARDSLEY & WOLCOTT MFG. CO.

Torrid, mid-early 1930s, 7⅛" high, chrome plated body with black wooden handles, no heat control. Marked on the bottom "Torrid Cat. Series No. T-70 Volts 115 Watts 500 The Beardsley and Wolcott Mfg. Co. Waterbury Conn." $45.00.

BEE-VAC

late 1920s, 8½" high, nickel plated body with wooden handles and fiber feet. Nameplate reads "Bee-Vac Toaster No. T12 Watts 625 AT 115V Volts 110 to 120 Birtman Electric Company. Chicago." Note: The Russel patented wire frame inside the door does not release the toast, rather the Rutenber moving grill launches the toast down and out. $55.00.

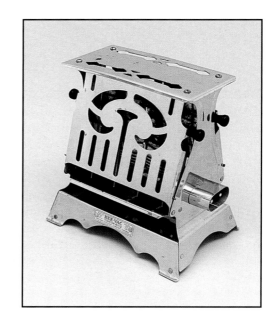

BERSTED

1926 – 1928, 7" high, chrome plated body and base, black wooden handles on one side of each of the doors, fiber feet, no heat control, the laced coil heating element is laced through a ceramic rod on the top and bottom. Nameplate on side reads: "Bersted Electric Toaster Mfd. By Bersted Mfg. Co. Chicago Ill. 110 Volts 475 Watts Serial No. 1." The top of the doors do not have a turned over top to catch the bread when pulled down for turning, therefore the doors have to be held in position while bread is being turned manually. $45.00.

BERSTED

1930, 7¼" high, chrome plated body with black Bakelite handles and wafer feet, manually operated, spring operated flip down doors. Marked on the bottom: "Bersted Model No. 71 115V 400 W. Bersted Mfg. Co. Fostoria, Ohio." $30.00.

BERSTED

1930s, 7¼" high, chrome plated body with Bakelite carrying and door handles, no heat control. Marked on the bottom: "Bersted Mfg By Bersted Mfg. Co. Fostoria. O. Model No. 72 Watts 400 Volts 115." $50.00.

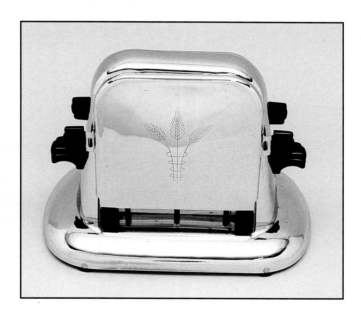

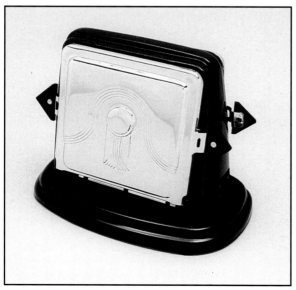

BERSTED

1930s, 7¼" high, chrome plated doors with black body and base. Marked on the bottom: "Bersted Model No. 66 115V 400W Bersted Mfg. Co. Fostoria, Ohio." $30.00.

BERSTED
Late 1930s, 7½" high, chrome plated body with Bakelite carrying and door handles, no heat control. Marked on the bottom: "Bersted Model No. 68 115V 400W Bersted Mfg. Co. Fostoria, Ohio." $45.00.

BERSTED MFG. CO.
Victorian 4 Slice, late 1930s, 6⅜" high, chrome plated doors with black "baked-on" enamel painted top, sides, and base, Bakelite handles, 4-section mica heating element, no heat control. Marked on the bottom: "Victorian Mfg. by Bersted Mfg. Co. Model No. A55 Watts 750 Volts 115 Pat. Pending." $45.00.

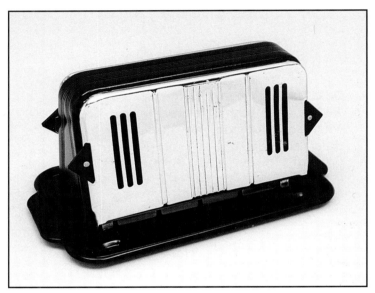

BERSTED
1930s, 7⅜" high, with original cord and box. Chrome body with brown wooden handles, no heat control. Toaster marked on bottom: "Fostoria, Mfd. By Bersted Mfg. Co. Fostoria, O. Model No. 67, Watts 400 Volts 115." $35.00 w/cord. $85.00 w/cord and box.

BERSTED MFG. CO.

Fostoria, early 1930s, 7" high, chrome body, fiber door pulls and carrying handles. Marked on the bottom: "Fostoria, Made By Bersted Mfg. Co. Fostoria O. Model No. 80 Watts 450. Volts 115." $65.00.

BERSTED MFG. CO.

Fostoria 4 Slice Toaster, 1940s, 6⅞" high, chrome body and base with Bakelite door handles, base, carrying handles, and feet, 4-section mica heating element, no heat control. Marked on the bottom: "Fostoria Bersted Mfg. Co. Fostoria, 0. 115 Volt 750 Watt Model No. 60 Pat. Pending." $65.00.

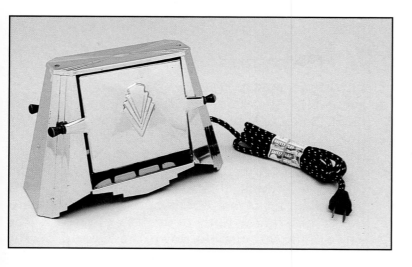

CAN FITZGERALD LTD.

Fitzgerald Ltd., 1930s, 7⅜" high, chrome plated body with black wooden handles, no heat control. Marked on the bottom: "500W H.E.P.C. 853 115V Cat 525C Can Fitzgerald Ltd." Note: The original wrapper is on the "Safety-Plus" cord set. Wrapper reads: "Safety-Plus 6 ft. No. 706 Rodale Manufacturing Company Inc. Emmaus, Pennsylvania." $125.00.

TOASTERS

CALKINS APPLIANCE CO.

Breakfaster, 1930s, 5" high, combination toaster/hotplate, has vented sides, black Bakelite handles and base. Marked on bottom: "Calkins Appliance Co. Niles, Michigan USA. Model T2 Break- faster Volts 115 Watts 750." When the front door is pulled down, the attached toast rack comes forward to place bread on for toasting. There are no heat controls for the hotplate or toaster. $75.00 w/cord.

CALKINS APPLIANCE CO.

Breakfaster, 1930, 5" high. Shown here how two things can be accomplished at one time. Toast door is shown in open position to show where bread is put in for toasting as well as heating a beverage on the top of the Breakfaster. $75.00. (Cof- fee pot shown here is Granite Ware.)

CANADIAN TOASTESS

late 1930s, 6⅜" high, high lustre chrome body with black Bakelite handles, mica heat- ing element, no heat control. Marked "SA 115V. 400W Model 201 Toastess Corpora- tion. Made In Canada." $25.00.

CANADIAN MERIT-MADE

late 1930s, 8¼" high, chrome body and base with black Bakelite handles, wafer feet, no heat con- trol. Marked on the bottom: "Patent Applied For. Merit Made Forterie, CNI Made In Canada. Model Z 115 Volts 475 Watts CSAAPP No. 76199." Note: Unlike the others, this toaster does not have the top pull-up lever that opens both doors simultane- ously, but rather both doors are opened at the same time by pushing down the handle on the right. The other handle is stationary. $75.00.

CANADIAN-WESTINGHOUSE

1914 – 1920s, 7⅛" high, highly polished nickel body with mica heating elements and molded metal feet. Nameplate on the side reads: "Turnover Toaster Canadian Westinghouse Co. Limited. Hamilton. Canada. Patented Feb. 1914. May 1915. Volts 105/115 STYLE H18010A. Amps 5 BW-1." The flat open design on top of the toaster is marked: "Westinghouse." $40.00.

CANADIAN WESTINGHOUSE

1930s, 7" high, chrome plated body with black Bakelite handles and feet. Marked on the lower left side "Westinghouse." Marked on the bottom: "Canadian Westinghouse Co. Limited Model TH25 No. H50225 115 V 620 W C.S.A. Approved No. 27 Pat 1936." When the front and back handles are pushed down at the same time, this pushes the toast rack up for the toast to be removed manually. $50.00.

CANADIAN WESTINGHOUSE

late 1930s, 6¾" high, chrome plated body with Bakelite handles and feet, mica heating element, no heat control. Marked on the bottom: "Canadian Westinghouse Co. Limited, Hamilton Canada Model TT-2-S #H50185 115V 400W CSA Approval No. 27." $30.00.

CANADIAN WESTINGHOUSE

1930s, 8" high, chrome body with black fancy Bakelite door pulls and fiber feet, mica core heating element. Marked on the bottom: "Canadian Westinghouse Hamilton, Canada. S#H27389-A 110V 550W C.E.S.A. Approval No. 27." $45.00.

CAPITOL

mid 1930s, 7¼" high, chrome body with wooden handles. Marked on the bottom: "Cat No. 50 UL Capitol Prods. Winsted Conn. Made In USA 500 Watts 120 Volts." No heat control. $30.00.

CAPITOL

1930s, 7¼" high, brown "baked-on" enamel painted body with nickel plated doors and wooden handles. Marked on the bottom: "Cat No. 50 Capitol Prod. Winsted, Conn. Made In USA 500 Watts 120 Volts." $30.00.

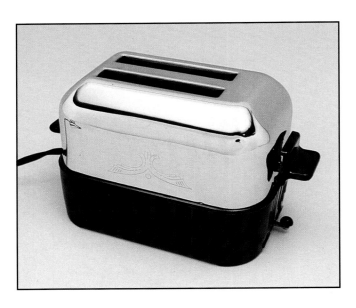

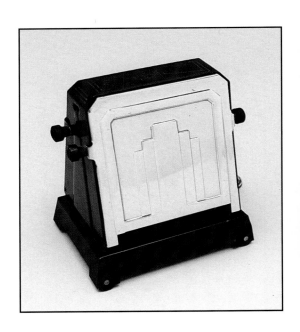

CAPITOL

late 1940s, 6⅝" high, chrome plated body with black Bakelite handles and base, light and dark heat control lever, pops toast up automatically. Marked on bottom: "Capitol Products Co. Inc. Winsted, Conn. 800 Watts 115 Volts AC Only Made In USA Model No. 555 UL Pop-up." $35.00.

CHALLENGE

late 1920s, 7½" high, chrome doors with black painted top, base, and wooden knobs, wafer feet, mica element w/no controlled heat. Bottom marked: "Challenge 450 Watts 110 Volts 1860 Cat. 307." $30.00.

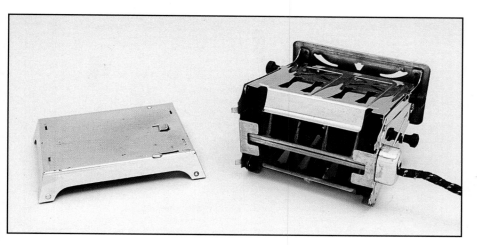

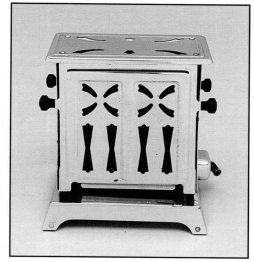

CHALLENGE

1930s, 7⅞" high with base, chrome plated body with black wooden handles and wafer feet, no heat control. Marked on the bottom: "E10552 Challenge 525 Watts 110 Volts Cats. 797 Pat. Appld. For." On the right front side of the base is a lever that when pushed to the left "open" position the toaster can be removed from the base for cleaning. When toaster is then replaced on the base, the lever is pushed to the right to the "lock" position to secure the toaster to the base. $65.00.

CHALLENGE

1930s, 7⅞" high, chrome plated body with black wooden handles. Marked on the bottom: "E10552 Challenge 525 Watts 110 Volts Cat. 5797." The open and lock lever is embossed "Pat Appld. For." Note: The different cut-outs on the door and top. $65.00.

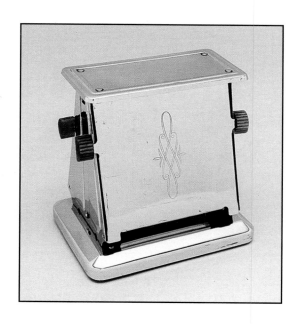

CHALLENGE

manufacturer unmarked, 1930s, 7⅝" high, chrome plated body with walnut handles, no heat control. Marked on the bottom: "Challenge Volts 110-120 AC or DC Watts 550 No. 307-6301." $35.00.

CHICAGO ELECTRIC MFG. CO.

Chicago Electric, 1920s, 6⅝" high, nickel plated body with fiber handles and feet, no heat control. Marked on the bottom: "Chicago Electric Mfg. Co. Chicago Ill. 110 Volts 560 Watts." $35.00.

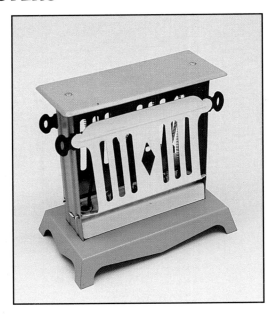

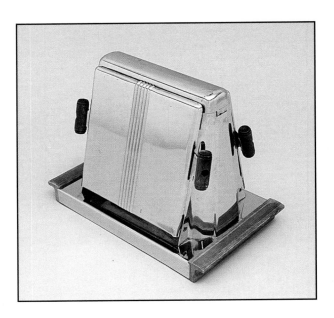

CHICAGO ELECTRIC MFG. CO.

Handyhot, 1920s, 7" high, painted green and cream enamel, black wafer handles. Marked on bottom: "Handyhot, Chicago Electric Mfg. Co. Chicago IL 110 Volts 500 Watts Patents Pending." The heating elements are laced open spring coil. This toaster was never used. $65.00.

CHICAGO ELECTRIC MFG. CO.

Handyhot, late 1930s, 7" high, chrome plated body with black wooden carrying and door handles, no heat control. Marked on the bottom: "Handyhot 110-120 Volts 400 Watts Chicago Electric Mfg. Co. Type AEUS Made In USA Patented Model 589." $30.00.

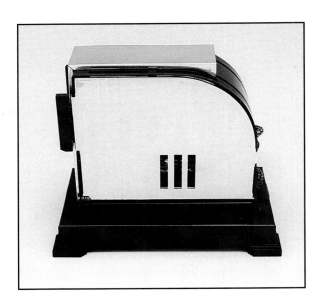

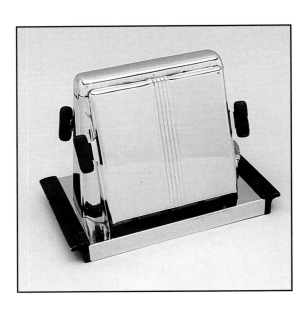

CHICAGO ELECTRIC MFG. CO.

Handyhot, 1930s, 7½" high, chrome plated doors and top with black painted base and side, Bakelite handles and feet. Marked on the bottom: "105-115 Volts 500 Watts Patent Pending AEUB Handyhot, Chicago Electric Mfg. Co. Made in the USA." $175.00.

CHICAGO ELECTRIC MFG. CO.

Handyhot, late 1930s, 7" high, chrome plated body with walnut carrying handles and door handles, no heat control. Marked on the bottom: "Handyhot 110-120 Volts 400 Watts Chicago Electric Mfg. Co. Type AEUS Made in USA Patented Model 589." Note: I believe these toasters could be ordered according to the color of the carrying and door handles, as you can see by the different examples shown. $30.00.

CHICAGO ELECTRIC MFG. CO.
Sterling, 1930s, 7⅛" high, chrome plated doors with "baked-on" enamel painted body, wooden handles. Marked on the bottom: "Sterling 110-120 Volts 660 Watts Chicago Electric Mfg. Co. Pat No. 1,987,356. Type AEUE Made In USA." $45.00.

CHICAGO ELECTRIC MFG. CO.
Victory, 1930s, 7¼" high, chrome doors and upper part of base, with black painted body panels, vertically laced open spring coil heating element. Marked on the bottom: "Victory Brand. Chicago Electric Mfg. Co. Chicago Ill. 105-120 Volts 500 Watts. A Handyhot Product. Patented No. 83830." Note this style is referred to as a "turner" or "flopper." $40.00.

CHICAGO ELECTRIC MFG. CO.
Victory, 1930s, 7½" high, chrome doors, top, and side panels with black painted frame and base, vertically laced open spring coil heating element. Marked on the bottom: "Victory Brand. 105-115 Volts. 500 Watts Chicago Electric Mfg. Co. Another Handyhot Product. Type AEU, Made In USA Patents Pending." This style toaster is referred to as a "turner" or "flopper." $35.00.

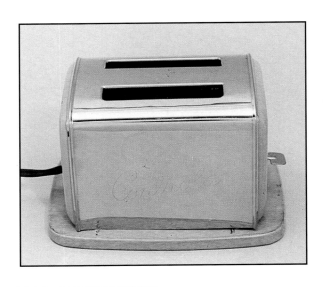

COMMON SENSE

early 1900s, 4" high, perforated tin with wire toast racks. Marked on top: "Common Sense Toaster Pat. Dec. 28, 09." $55.00.

CONTROLA TOY ELECTRIC

late 1950s, 3¾" x 5¾" high, nickel plated body with light brown painted sides, maker unknown. This toaster holds ½ slice of bread on each side. Both toast baskets are pushed down at once by the lever on the right side. The lever is held down by a small cut-out on the lower section of the toaster. No heat control. The lever has to be released manually when toast is done, and the toaster shuts off. $45.00.

CROCKER WHEELER ELECTRIC MFG. CO.,

Toast-O-Later, complete with original box and toaster tongs, late 1930 – 1940s. 9½" high, chrome body with black Bakelite base and handles. Serial No. 1039 Crocker Wheeler Electric Mfg. Co. Ampere, N.J. Paper label on bottom reads: "Crocker Wheeler Trademark Reg. U.S. Pat Office. Tested and Approved By Good Housekeeping Institute Conducted by *Good Housekeeping* Magazine Serial No. 3379." Note: The unique mechanism of this toaster. The bread is placed in the toaster on the right side, the bread then moves through the toaster and past the heating element on a conveyor type chain. The timing is controlled by a silent accurate electric motor. The exclusive Wind-O-Spy enables you to watch the bread move by as it is being toasted. Also note that the left side of the toaster base is rounded so the toast can drop down and out. This is where the toast tongs are used to catch the toast before it drops down and out. $275.00 without original box and tongs, $425.00 with box and tongs.

CURTAINLESS

Reddy Toaster Range, 1920s, 2⅝" high by 8¼" long and 4⅝" wide, nickel plated body with white porcelain feet, laced coil heating element, no heat control. Marked on the bottom: "Reddy Toaster Range Volt 110 AMP 4.4 Mfg. By Curtainless, New York Patent Pending." $25.00.

DELTA

Pop-Down Automatic, late 1930s – 1940s, 8⅞" high, chrome front, top and back with blue enamel painted sides, black Bakelite handles, heat control knob on the lower left side. Lower side of body is marked "D-L-Release." Marked on the bottom: "Delta Pop-Down Automatic Toaster Model 280. 110-120 Volts 940 Watts UL Underwriters Approved For AC Use Only. Delta Manufacturing Corporation Phila, Penna. USA Pats Pend." $300.00.

DELTA

Pop-Down Automatic, with original box, 1930s – 1940s, 8⅞" high, chrome body with black Bakelite handles and heat control knob. On the lower side of the body is marked "D-L-Release." Marked on the bottom: "Delta Pop-Down Automatic Toaster Model 280. 110-120 Volts 940 Watts UL Underwriters Approved For AC Use Only. Delta Manufacturing Corporation Phila, Penna. USA Pat. Pend." Note: The toast slots each measure 1" wide in the center and ¾" on each end. $250.00 with original box.

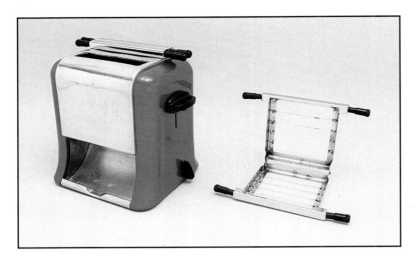

DELTA

Sandwich Toaster, complete With Two Sandwich Baskets, 1930s – 1940s, 8⅞" high with polished aluminum front, back and top, red enamel painted sides, black Bakelite handles and heat control knob. On the lever side of the toaster body is marked: "D-L Release." Marked on the bottom: "202222 Delta Model 300 Sandwich Toaster. 110-120 Volts 1140 Watts For AC Use Only. Delta Manufacturing Corporation Phila, Penna. USA Pats. Pending." Each sandwich basket holds one sandwich. Basket measures 4¾" square by 1" deep. The sandwich slot on the top of the toaster measures 1¼" wide and 4⅞" long. This is the only Delta sandwich toaster I have seen complete with the sandwich baskets. $300.00 without baskets and $400.00 complete.

DELTA

Sandwich, 1930s – 1940s, 8⅞" high, chrome body with black Bakelite handles and heat control knob. The lower left side of the body is marked "D-L-Release." Marked on the bottom: "203970 Delta Model 300 Sandwich Toaster 110-120 Volts 1140 Watts For AC Use Only. Delta Manufacturing Corporation Phila, Penna. USA Pats Pending," stamped with black numbers "53-49," also has part of a "UL" sticker. This toaster is designed to hold two sandwich baskets. The slots measure 1¼" wide, 4⅞" long, slots are not tapered on each end. $175.00.

DEREE

late 1930s, 7" high, brown rough textured body and base, and light brown tinted doors, with an Art Deco style decoration, brown Bakelite handles, mica heating element, no heat control. Marked on the bottom: "115V AC/DC 475 Watts Model 1 Deree Co. Chgo. UL." $30.00.

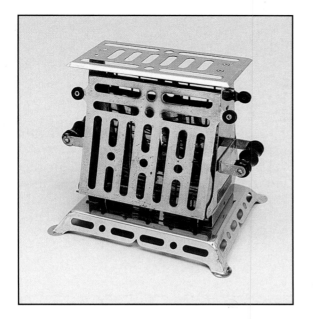

DOMINION MFG. CO.

Lady, late 1920s, 7⅞" high, nickel plated body with wooden carrying handles and fiber handles, no heat control. Side label reads: "Dominion Lady Volts 110-120 Dependable Domino Devices Watts 550 Style 50 Dominion Electrical Mfg. Co. Minneapolis, USA." $65.00.

DOMINION MFG. CO.

Sandwich, late 1930s, chrome body with porcelain insert, decorated with a floral decoration, heat control indicator, brown Bakelite carrying handles and cover handle, fiber feet. Marked on the bottom: "Style No. 532 Volts 110-120 Watts 660. Dominion Elec. Mfg. Co. Mansfield, Ohio." $125.00.

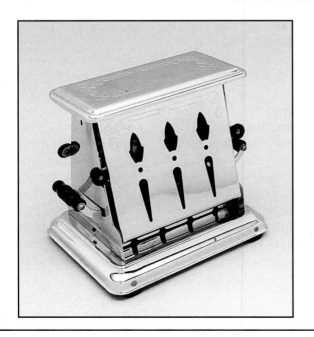

DOMINION MFG. CO.

late 1920s, 7¼" high, chrome body with wooden carrying handles, fiber feet, mica heating element. Marked on the bottom: "Dominion Electrical Mfg. Co. Minneapolis, Minn. Dependable Domino Services. Style 47 Patent No. 1,105,230 Volts 110-120 Watts 550. $55.00.

DOMINION MFG. CO.

late 1920s, 7½" high, nickel plated body with black wooden carrying handles, fiber door handles and feet, no heat control. Marked on the bottom: "Volts 110-120 Watts 510 Dependable Domino Services. Style 48 Patent No. 1,105,330. Dominion Electrical Mfg. Co Minneapolis, Minn." $55.00.

DOMINION MFG. CO.

1940s, 7½" high, chrome body with walnut handles, light and dark control signal bell. Marked on the bottom: "Style No. 1105 Watts 660 Volts 110-120 AC Only. Dominion Electrical Mfg. Inc. Mansfield Ohio USA." $50.00.

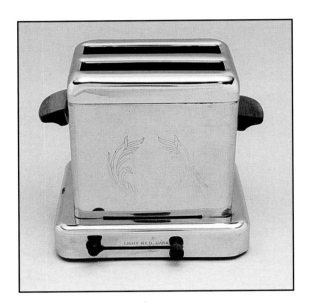

DOMINION MFG. CO.

1930s, 8⅜" high, nickel plated body, with wooden handles and knobs and wafer feet. Bottom nameplate reads "Volts 110 Dependable Domino Devices Watts 550, Dominion Electrical Mfg. Co. Minneapolis, Minn." First you set the browning lever, then you push the timing lever back to close the two side doors, then you put the bread in the tilted toaster baskets. The timing lever moves forward until the toast is done; it then clicks off, opening the two side doors automatically. The toast then tumbles out of the toaster down the elevated groove at the base of the toaster. $675.00.

DOMINION MFG. CO.
late 1930s, 7⅛" high, chrome body with black Bakelite handles and wooden concealed feet, mica heating element. Marked on the bottom: "Dominion, Dominion Electrical Co. Mansfield, Ohio. USA. Model No. 1109 Watts 450 Volts 110-120 H-8 (UL)." $35.00.

DOMINION MFG. CO.
late 1930s, 7⅛" high, chromium plated doors with painted black enamel body and base, wooden handles and feet, no heat control. Marked on the bottom: "Style #1101 Volts 110-120 Watts 450 Dominion Electrical Mfg. Inc., Mansfield, Ohio USA." $30.00.

DOMINION MFG. CO.
late 1930s, 7¼" high, chromium plated body with walnut handles and feet. Marked on the bottom: "Style #1103 Volts 110-120 Watts 450 Dominion Electrical Mfg. Inc. Mansfield, Ohio USA." Note: The "new" design doors will hold extra large slices of bread; when doors are lowered, toast flops over without being touched by hand. $25.00.

DOMINION MFG. CO.
mid 1930s, 7⅛" high, chrome finished doors with black top, sides, and base, wooden handles. Marked on the bottom: "Style No. 366 Volts 120 Watts 450, Dominion Mfg. Mansfield, Ohio." $40.00.

DOMINION MFG. CO.
1940s, 7½" high, chrome body with Bakelite handles and knobs, automatic pop-up, light and dark heat control with timer bell, shuts off automatically. Marked on the bottom: "Dominion Trademark Dominion Electric Corporation Mansfield, Ohio. USA. Model No. 1107-B 660 110-120 AC Only K-9." $50.00.

EDICRAFT
late 1920s – early 1930s, 7¾" high, nickel plated body with black Bakelite handles. Side nameplate reads: "Serial No. 2015 Reg US Pat. Office Thomas A. Edison Edicraft Automatic Toaster Made In USA Thomas A. Edison, Inc. Orange, NJ." Bottom is marked: "110 Volts - 660 Watts Patent No. 1,194,663 and Patents Pending." On the left side is a setting for open and closed numbered from 1-6. The lower front left has a timer button that is pushed to the left to start the toaster timing. Note: The unique feature of this toaster is when toast is done, it opens like a Morning Glory. It will also keep toast warm. $575.00.

ELECTRAHOT

late 1920s, 7" high, chrome body with black wooden carrying handles and Bakelite door pulls, wafer style feet, mica heating element, no heat control. Marked on the bottom: "Volts 110-120 Watts 500 Style No. 48 Manufactured By Electrahot Mfg. Co. Minneapolis, Minn." $50.00.

ELECTRAHOT

late 1920s, 7⅜" high, chrome plated doors with painted black enamel body and base, fiber handles, no heat control. Marked on the bottom: "Style No. 38 Volts 110-120 Watts 550 Electrahot Mfg. Co. Mansfield, Ohio." $30.00.

ELECTRAHOT

mid 1930s, 7¼" high, chrome plated body with fiber knobs, no heat control, mica heating element. Marked on the bottom: "Style No. 5115 Volts 110-120 Watts 550 Electrahot Mfg. Co. Mansfield, Ohio." This style is referred to as a "turner." $45.00.

ELECTRAHOT
late 1930s, 7⅛" high, chrome body with black wooden door handles and feet, mica heating element, no heat control. Marked on the bottom: "Style No. 618 Volts 110-120 Watts 450 Electrahot Mfg. Co. Mansfield, Ohio." $45.00.

ELECTRO AUTOMATIC
late 1920s – 1930s, 7½" high, chrome body with black wooden handle, and feet, front pullout crumb tray. Nameplate reads: "Electro Automatic Patents Pending 110 VOLTS 600 Watts Electro Mfg. Co. of America. No.1913 E9233, Phila., Pa., USA." When the timing lever on the right is pulled back, it pushes the two inner arms to back of the toaster; when bread is toasted, the timing lever pushes the two inner arms out against the toast. The toaster then shuts off automatically. The bread is laid directly on the wire that protects the heating elements. $275.00.

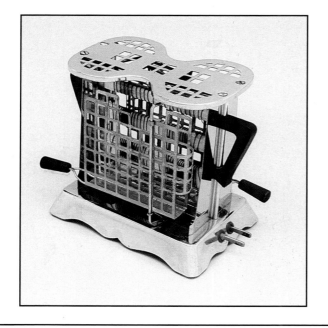

ELECTRO WELD CO.
1920s, 6½" high, chrome plated body with black wooden handles and knobs. The three ceramic cores are wrapped with a single wire and attached to the bottom section of the toaster through a ceramic fitter. No heat control. The base is weighted to keep it stabilized when in use. Marked on the bottom: "LMP Also Pat. Pend. Pat. Nov. 16, 1920 Electro Weld Co. Volts 110 Amps 5.5." $125.00.

ELECTRO WELD CO.

1920s, 6½" high, nickel plated body with orange wooden handles. The heating elements in this toaster are of interest; it has four separate mica panels, each measuring 1" wide. Marked on the bottom: "Pat. Nov. 16, 1920." This toaster has an off-on switch. The bread is placed in the open end of the toast basket, and when toast is done on one side, the toast basket is then swung out and around to toast the other side. This type toaster is referred to as a "swinger." $100.00.

ELECTRO WELD CO.

Reverso Electric, with original box and cord, 1920s, 6½" high, chrome body. Marked on the bottom: "Lmp. Pat. Pend. Pat. Nov. 16, 1920 Electro-Weld Co. Volts 110 Amps 5.5." Note: Each basket is attached at the top and base of the toaster by double arms that swing out and around for loading and toasting the other side. Baskets are separately and manually operated. There is a heavy weight on the base of this toaster to keep it stabilized. Also note the box reads: "Reverso Electric Toaster Lmp Pat, All'd Manufactured By The Electro-Weld Co. Lynn, Mass." It appears that this toaster has never been used. $125.00 with original box and cord.

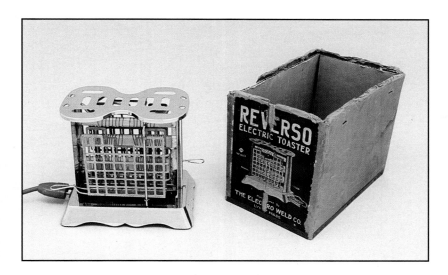

EMPIRE

1930s, 7" high, nickel plated body with black painted base and wooden handles and feet, mica heating element, no heat control. Marked on the bottom: "Empire The Metal Ware Corp. Two Rivers Wis. Made In USA 115 Volts 475 Watts. Cat No. 769. UL." $35.00.

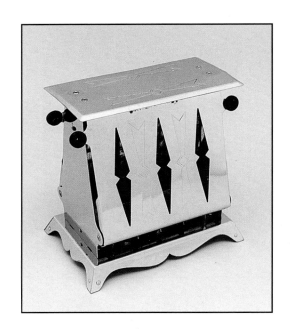

ENERGEX

1920s, 7¼" high, chrome body with fiber handles and feet. Marked on the bottom: "Energex Toaster Volts 110-120 Watts 520 (no manufacturer listed)." This could be a product of Royal Brand Products, New York, because the door designs are exactly like other toasters that are marked by Royal Brand Products of New York. $45.00.

ESTATE STOVE CO.

(at left in photo) early 1930s, 6½" high, nickel plated body with black wooden knobs and feet. Side nameplate reads: "Estate Electric Toaster No. 177 Volts 110 Amp 5.5 The Estate Stove Company Patents Pending." Bottom marked: "Patented June 27, 1911 April 14, 1925. Note: The four toaster baskets are hinged together, and pulling the knob on any one toaster basket will swing all four toaster baskets in

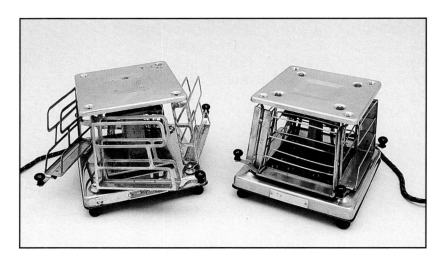

either direction which reverses the slices simultaneously. This toaster has the enclosed center post that fastens the upper section to the lower section of the toaster. The unusual mechanical mechanism was patented by Mr. Kahn in 1925. $200.00.

ESTATE STOVE CO.

(pictured above on right) early 1920s – 1930s, 6¾" high, nickel plated body with black wooden knobs and feet. Side nameplate reads: "Estate Electric Toaster Amp. 5.5 The Estate Stove Co. Hamilton, Ohio. Patents Pending. Note: This toaster is not numbered and doesn't tell the volts. Also note the differences in the four toaster baskets. This toaster has wire toaster baskets with one end open for bread to be placed in whereas the other end is closed. The inner center post is also different; it has two arms that support it and does not fasten to the top of the toaster compared to the one on the left. The four corner supporting rods fasten the top section to the bottom section. I believe this is the earlier of the two, because this still has patents pending whereas, the other has patent dates. $200.00.

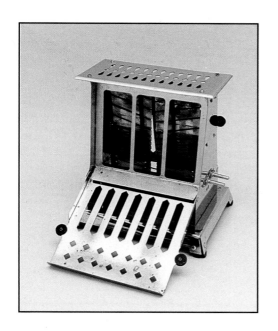

EV'RYDAY

late 1920s, 8" high, nickel plated body with wafer handles and feet, no heat control. Marked on the bottom: "Model No. 120 Ev'ryday Electric Co. Marion Ind. USA 110 Volt 550 Watts." We photographed this toaster open to show the added toast basket, which moves the bread out from the heating element. In most other toasters, the bread rests against stationary wires. $45.00.

THE EXTRUSION CO.

Reflecto, stove-top non-electric, early 1900s, 4¾" high by 8¾" diam., heavy gauge metal with nickel plated reflector. Marked: "Reflecto Toaster Patent Pend. The Extrusion Co. Manitowoc, WI, USA." Instructions are also marked on the toaster, "Raise wires 1-2-3-4-5, fold wires 5-4-3-2-1." Each wire is numbered on the base. This 3-slice stove-top toaster is unique in the fact that it has the reflector that reflects heat toward the bread. $35.00.

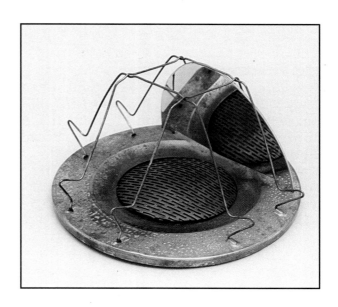

THE FITZGERALD MFG. CO.

Star-Rite Automatic Toaster, 1930s, 7¼" high, chrome body with black Bakelite handles, feet, and timing knob, dark and light heat control. When the light and dark heat control is set, the timing knob is pulled forward; when bread is toasted, the timing knob swings back and shuts toaster off. Toast is manually released sideways. Nameplate on the side reads: "Star-Rite, Made in the USA. Automatic Toaster. Cat. No. 529 CP Watts 880 Volts 115. The Fitzgerald Mfg. Co. Torrington Conn. Licensed Under Strite Pat No. 1,387.670". $145.00.

THE FITZGERALD MFG. CO.

Star-Rite, 1925 – 1930, 7⅜" high, chrome plated body with green wooden handles and fiber feet, laced wire coil heating element, no heat control. Marked on the bottom: "Star-Rite Extra Fast Toaster, Volts 105-115 Amps 5 The Fitzgerald Mfg. Co. Torrington, Conn. USA." Each door has only one handle on opposite sides. This toaster was made to be inexpensive, and is one of the last "pinchers" made. $35.00.

THE FITZGERALD MFG. CO.

Star-Rite Oven, 1930s, 7¼" high, chrome body with Bakelite handles and feet, off and on switch, mica heating element, no heat control. Side nameplate reads: "Star-Rite Oven Toaster. Made in USA Cat. No. 530 Watts 660 Volts 115. The Fitzgerald Mfg. Co. Torrington, Conn. Use Only With Base Or Wall Receptacle H.E.P.C. Appr No. 853-28. $135.00.

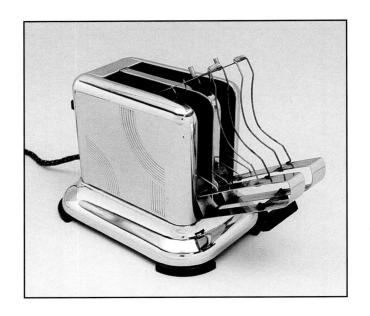

THE FITZGERALD MFG. CO.

Star-Rite Reversible Toaster, late 1920s – early 1930s, 8¾" high, chrome body. Marked on the bottom: "Star Electric Toaster, Patented. 105-115 Volts 550 Watts Manufactured By Fitzgerald Mfg. Co. Torrington, Conn. 75,000." The side carrying handles are embossed "Star-Rite". The hat type knobs on top are also marked "Star-Rite Fitzgerald Mfg. Co. USA." The doors are attached on the top and bottom of the toaster by an arm, each door can be swung out and around separately and manually for loading or toasting. Because of the imitation engraving, this toaster is considered Rare. $95.00.

THE FITZGERALD MFG. CO.

Star-Rite Reversible Toaster, with original box, cord and socket plug, late 1920s – early 1930s, 8¾" high, polished nickel body. Marked on the bottom: "Star Electric Toaster Patented 105-115 Volts 550W Manufactured By Fitzgerald Mfg. Co. Torrington Conn. 75,000". Note: The hat type knobs on the top of the toaster are marked "Star-Rite Toaster Fitzgerald Mfg. Co USA." $125.00 with original box, cord and socket plug.

THE FITZGERALD MFG. CO.

Star-Rite Sandwich, 1929, 6¼" high, chrome plated body with black Bakelite cover handle, carrying handles, and fancy scroll feet, off and on switch on lower right side. Marked on the bottom: "Star-Rite Sandwich Toaster Watts 450 Volts 110 Cat No. 528, Pat. No. 78839 June 25, 1929. The Fitzgerald Mfg. Co. Torrington, Conn. Made In USA." $125.00.

FRANKE WOLCOTT MFG. CO.

Torrid Pushomatic, 1920s, 6⅞" high, chrome plated body with red wooden carrying knobs, and red Bakelite push knobs. Marked on bottom: "Torrid 5.7 Amps 110 Volts Hartford, Conn The Franke Wolcott. Mfg. Co. Pat'd. Nov. 15, 1920 Feb. 15, 1927." Note: A similar toaster pictured on page 12 has mica heating elements whereas, this toaster has the laced coil heating element. These toast baskets are each operated by a push button on the side of the toaster. Below each carrying handle, on each side is a fast and slow lever, these control the speed of the basket when turned as well as the distance of the basket from the heating element, which determines the crispness of the toast. This is one of two pushomatics known; the other is the Landers, Frary & Clark Universal E9410 shown on page 54. $250.00.

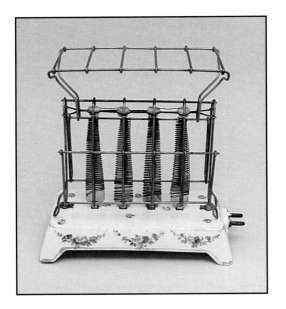

GENERAL ELECTRIC

D-12, early 1900s, 6¾" high without toast rack, with toast rack 8½" high, white porcelain base decorated with a floral pattern. Marked on bottom: "Pat. Oct. 20, 1908. Patent Applied For G.E. Co. USA Type D-12 A.V." Note: The patent date of October 20, 1908 refers to the resistance wire alloys containing iron with which GE hoped to evade Marshe's patent. The porcelain base was patented 1909 – 1910. The porcelain base also serves as an ideal insulator against electricity and heat. This is the second version of the D-12 with the high toast basket. The first version has the enclosed ends of the toast baskets, whereas, this version has open ends on the toast baskets. The floral decoration on the base was optional at an extra cost. Price without toast rack $800.00. Price with toast rack $875.00.

GENERAL ELECTRIC

D-12, Note: This is also the second version of the D-12 with the six frame structure without the floral decorated base. We have pictured the removable toast rack off the toaster so you could see how it is applied by snapping the wire prongs over the top wires of the toaster. $450.00 with toast rack.

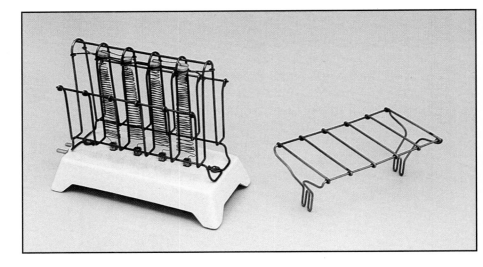

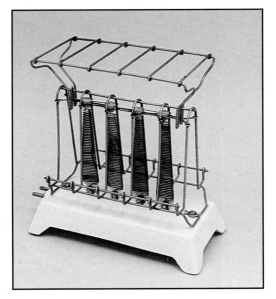

GENERAL ELECTRIC

D-12, early 1900s, 6¾" high without toast rack, 8½" high with toast rack, white porcelain base. Marked: "Pat. Oct. 20, 1908. Dec. 28, 1909. G.E. Co. USA Type D-12 A.V." Note: This is the third version, the sides of the toast baskets are much lower. Toast can be tipped straight out. In comparison the revision carries two patents; this is because of another experimental heating element. Their alloy was called "Calorite" as mentioned in an ad from a 1912 *Good Housekeeping.* Presumably with the exception of the 1915 X-2, this is the last toaster G.E. made until after World War I, when they brought out "Hotpoint." $375.00 with toast rack.

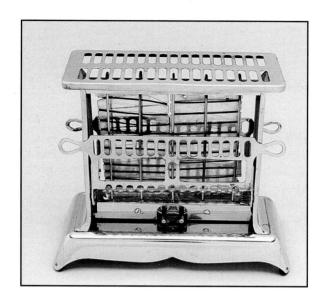

GENERAL ELECTRIC

1909 – 1910, 7¾" high, nickel plated body with wafer feet, mica heating element, no heat control. Marked on the bottom: "Pat Dec. 29, 1909. Feb. 22, 1910 G.E. Co. USA Type D72 V110 A.5.0." Etched on the bottom, "55MB." This could possibly be the initials of the person who made this toaster, along with the quantity produced. $125.00.

GENERAL ELECTRIC

Toaster and Sandwich Toaster, late 1930s, 7⅝" high, chrome body with Bakelite door pulls, mica heating element, no heat control. Marked on the bottom: "General G.E. Electric Volts 115 Cat No. 119T48 Watts 450 General Electric Co. Bridgeport Conn. Made In USA Ontario, Calif." Note: The bottom section of each door has a plate marked "Expand Hinge For Toasting Sandwiches." These hinges are made so the doors are pulled out farther away from the bottom of the toaster, allowing room for a sandwich to fit in the door. $50.00.

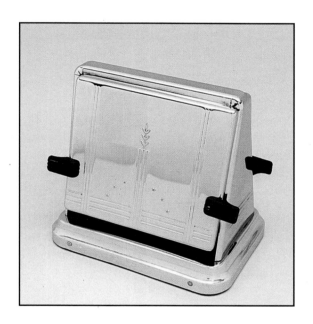

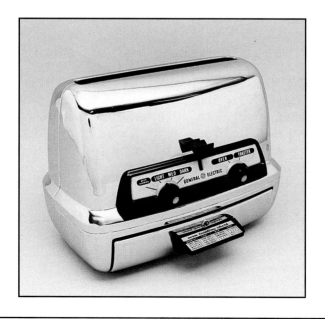

GENERAL ELECTRIC

Toaster and Toaster Oven Combination, late 1940s, 9⅝" high, chrome plated body with black Bakelite knobs and feet, automatic toaster, toaster oven door pulls out for warming or toasting, door has heat control light. Marked on the bottom: "General Electric Cat No. 85T83, 120 Volts 1200 Watts. Bridgeport Conn. Made In USA UL AC Only." $75.00.

GENERAL ELECTRIC
1940s, 7¼" high, chrome plated body with black Bakelite handles, wafer feet, no heat control. Marked on the bottom: "General G.E. Electric Volts 115 Cat. No. 119T46 Watts 450 General Electric Co. Bridgeport Conn. Made In USA Ontario Calif." $65.00.

GENERAL MILLS
Automatic Pop-Up, late 1940s, 7⅞" high, chrome body with Bakelite handles and base, red light and dark control knob. Marked on the bottom: "General Mills Automatic Pop-up Toaster. Manufactured by General Mills Inc. Minneapolis, Minn. USA. (several patent numbers listed) 110-120 Volts 1200 Watts Cat No. GM5A No. MG Operates on AC or DC UL." $40.00.

GIRARD
early 1900s, 6¾" high. The metal structure of the body is tin with an enamel paint finish. Marked on the bottom in a circle: "Girard Toaster Guaranteed, 110 Volts 500 Watts." Note: Each wire door is manually operated by pulling one of the knobs down. The bread is turned manually for browning on the other side. The little spring between the two door knobs holds the door closed. The criss-cross support wires hold the bread away from the heating elements. $85.00.

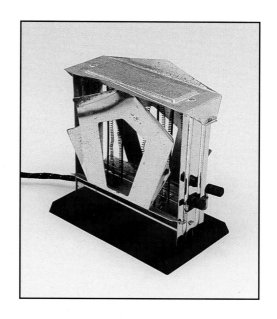

GIRARD

early 1930s, 6⅞" high, chrome body with painted black base. Marked on the bottom: "Girard Toaster Guaranteed 110 Volts 500 Watts." This toaster has vertical support wires that keep the toast from coming in direct contact with the laced coil heating element. Each door is operated separately and manually by pulling one of the spring-loaded knobs down. No heat control. $95.00.

GOLD SEAL ELECTRIC CO.

early 1920s, 7" high, nickel plated body with black wooden handles, laced spring-coil heating element. Nameplate reads: "The Gold Seal Electric Co. Cleveland, Ohio. Trademark Quality, Value, Service. Volts 110 No. 10469." No heat control, each door is turned over manually. This type toaster is called a "side-winder." $95.00.

GOLD SEAL ELECTRIC CO.

1920s, 6⅞" high, nickel body with black wooden handles and feet. Marked on the bottom in a circle: "The Gold Seal Electric Co. Cleveland O. Quality, Value, Service Trademark." No model number. This type is referred to as a "side-winder." Bread is slid into the open end of the toast basket. By using the black knob, the toast basket is then flipped over to toast the other side. $95.00.

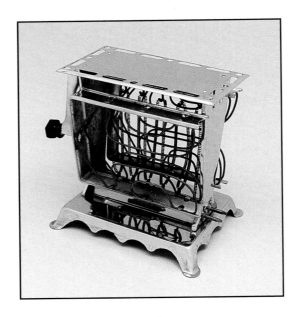

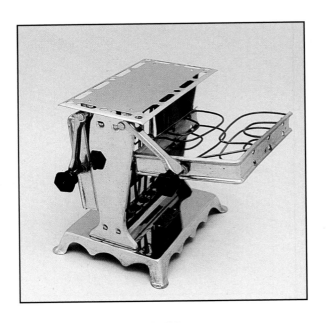

GOLD SEAL ELECTRIC CO.

1920s, 8¼" high, nickel plated body with black wooden handles. Nameplate reads: "The Gold Seal Electric Co. Cleveland Ohio, Volts 110 No. 40809. (marked in a circle) Quality, Value, Service Trademark." $125.00.

GOLD SEAL ELECTRIC CO.

previous toaster shown in open position. Bread is slid into the open end of the toast basket. By using the black knob, the toast basket is then flipped over to toast the other side. This type toaster is called a "side-winder." $125.00.

TOASTESS CORPORATION

(left), Toastess, 6¼" high, late 1930s. High lustre chrome body with black Bakelite handles. Marked on bottom: "SA 125V – 450W listed UL 708M Model – 202. Toastess Corporation, Montreal, Canada." Toaster is complete with original cord and box. $80.00.

H&S PRODUCTS

(right), Toaster, marked "Model 202 400W-115V S. A. App. No. 7490 H&S Products Montreal, Canada." This toaster has black wooden handles instead of Bakelite. There are no heat controls on either. The toast has to be removed manually. Neither toaster has a power switch. Without box $30.00.

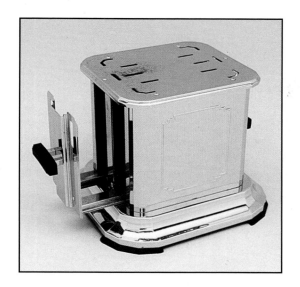

HEATMASTER

1930s, 6¾" high, chrome body with Bakelite handles and feet, no heat control, laced coil heating element. Marked on the bottom: "Heatmaster No. 690 Volts 110-120 Watts 660 Pats 1,466,656 1,820, 885." Note: Door is operated manually by pulling door out, placing a slice of bread on each rack, and pushing the door in to toast. After toasting, pull door open to release toast. Notice that the rack has no side supports so that when the door is opened the toast could fall off sideways. $110.00

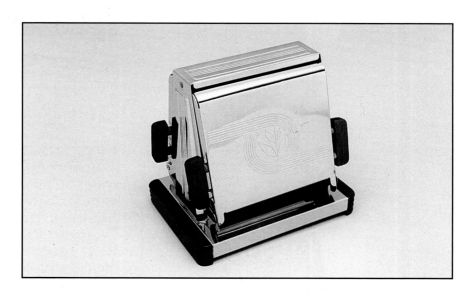

HEATMASTER

1930s, 7¼" high, chrome body with walnut handles and elongated feet, no heat control. Marked on the bottom: "Heatmaster Watts 500 Volts 110-120 Stock No. 2021. Model No. 281-1027584. Made In USA UL." This toaster has no manufacturer listed on the bottom, but I believe this could be a product of the McGraw Electric Company, Toastmaster Products Division, Minneapolis, Minn. $40.00.

HEATMASTER

1930s, 7½" high, chrome plated body with walnut handles, Bakelite knobs, light and dark heat control. Marked: "Heatmaster Model No. 307 Volts 110-120 Watts 660 A.C. only." No manufacturer is marked but toaster is similar to one in Sept. 26, 1938 Dominion catalog. $55.00.

HEATMASTER

mid 1930s, 7⅛" high, chrome doors and base with black painted top and sides, black Bakelite door handles and wafer feet, mica heating element, no heat control. Marked on the bottom: "696 Heatmaster 110-120 Volts 500 Watts C-33." $35.00.

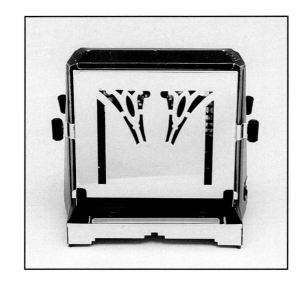

HILCO ENG. CO.

Volcano Roaster-Toaster, with original box, 1930s, 5⅝" high, chrome body with black wooden handles. Marked on the side: "Volcano Pat. Pend. Trademark Reg. Hilco Eng. Co. Chicago. MOD2000 115V 550W." Note: The grid on top of the toaster can be raised ½" to 1" with the lever on the side that fits into two different height slots. This method controls the roasting or toasting heat, as there is no controlled heat indicator on this unit. $85.00 with original box.

HOTPOINT

late 1920s, 7⅞" high, polished nickel body. Marked on lower section of the base: "Hotpoint." Marked on bottom: "Cat. No. 127T23 W625 V110 Pat. Apr. 1, 1924, Feb. 22, 1910, July 28, 1914 Edison Electric Appliance Co. Inc. Chicago Made in USA Ontario, Cal." Note: The 1928 Edison Electric Appliance Co. Inc. catalog refers to this toaster as an ornamental Toast-over Toaster. The pattern is called Princess. When the sides are lowered, the toast turns automatically. Artistically pierced sides and top, cool metal handles, and open coil heating unit. $45.00.

HOTPOINT

with original box and socket plug, 1910 – 1920s, 7⅞" high, polished nickel finish. Marked on the lower section of the base "Hotpoint." Marked on the bottom: "Cat. No. 115T17 W550 V110 Pat'd Feb 22, 1910, July 28, 14 Edison Electric Appliance Co. Inc. Chicago Made in USA Ontario, Cal." The 1928 Edison Electric Appliance Co. Inc. catalog refers to this toaster as the Deluxe Toast-Over Toaster 115T17, with switch plug, polished nickel finish with ornamental piercing on sides, ends, and tops. Semi-concealed non-scratch fiber feet, detachable plug, mica-core heating unit. It will toast large size slices which are turned automatically when the sides are lowered. Note: Toasters found with original boxes and original plug accessories and never used usually demand a premium price, especially the older ones. Also, the condition, age, and amount of advertising on the box as well as the condition of the toaster make a considerable difference in pricing. $125.00.

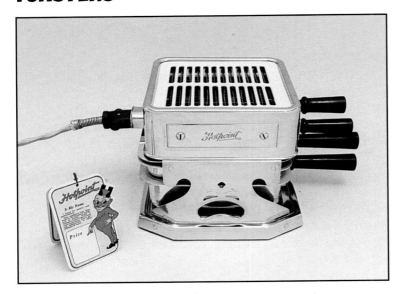

HOTPOINT

Triplex Grill, 1928, 6¾" high, chrome plated body with white enamel grill top, ebonized wooden handles and concealed fiber feet, standard attachment cord and separate plug. Marked on top side: "Hotpoint." Marked on the bottom: "Cat. No. 116G10 Watts 660 Volts 110 Patented Nov. 4, 13 Edison Electric Appliance Co. Inc. Chicago Made in USA Ontario, Calif." Note: The little Hotpoint man advertising explains the use of this appliance. $200.00 with Hotpoint man advertisement.

HOTPOINT

Triplex Grill, same as pictured above, shown apart. Lower left: toasting rack. Upper left: egg poacher. Lower right: shallow pan. Upper right: deep pan with insert. This unit will prepare a meal for two, three, or even four people at one time. $175.00 without Hotpoint man advertisement.

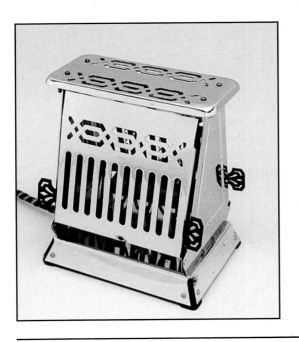

HOTPOINT

late 1920s, 7⅞" high, nickel finish with black enamel painted handles. Marked on the side of base: "Hotpoint." Marked on the bottom: "General GE Electric Cat. No. Hotpoint Volts 115 Watts 660. 159T25 Patents General Electric Co. Bridgeport Conn Ontario Calif." Note: This toaster has the laced spring coiled element and the non-scratching semi-concealed fiber feet. An ad states "Golden brown toast from the largest size loaf of bread." $40.00.

HOTPOINT
1930s, 7¼" high, chrome doors with black frame and base, Bakelite handles. Marked on the bottom: "General Electric Cat. No. 119T45 Hotpoint Volts 115 Watts 450 General Electric Co. Bridgeport Conn USA Ontario Calif." $25.00.

HOTPOINT
1923 – 1929, 8" high, chrome body with black knobs. Marked on the bottom: "B33 General Electric, Hotpoint. Cat No. 119T17 Volts 115 Watts 550 General Electric Co. Bridgeport Conn Ontario Calif." Also marked on the outer right edge of the base is "Hotpoint." This toaster has a paneled mica heating element. Each door is operated separately and manually by turning the black wooden knobs on the lower section of the doors. $45.00.

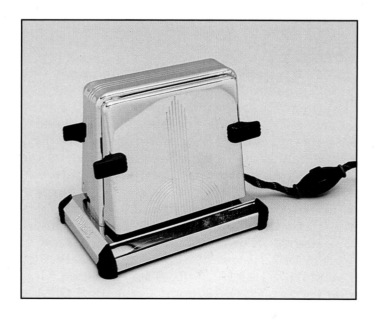

HOTPOINT
1930s, 7" high, chrome body with black Bakelite handles and feet, on and off heat control switch attached to the cord. Marked on the bottom: "Cat. No. T19-400W-115V Canadian General Electric Co. Limited, Toronto, Canada H.E.P.C. App No. 336." $30.00.

TOASTERS

HOTPOINT

1930s, 6⅞" high, chrome body with black Bakelite handles, knobs, and base. Base marked "Hotpoint." Marked on the bottom: "Cat. 129 T-31 Watts 525, Volt 115 Made in USA Edison Pats. 1551336 General GE Electric Appliance Company, Inc. Chicago Ill. Ontario Calif." Note: The browning dial at the base of the toaster is lettered from "A" to "K". When set for desired browning and browning is completed, the toaster shuts off automatically. The toast basket lever is then manually pulled down towards you and the toast tilts out. The lever is then pushed back to close the door. $525.00.

HOTPOINT

1930s, 7⅞" high, polished nickel finish. Marked on lower section of base "HOTPOINT." Marked on the bottom: "Cat. 159T26 Watts 600 Volts 115 Pats 1105230 Made in USA By Edison General Electric Appliance Company Inc. Chicago Ill. Ontario Calif." Note: Both doors are flipped down at once by manually turning the open and close knob on the side of the toaster; this method is then repeated for toasting the other side. We have shown both views to show the laced coil heating unit. Toaster on the right is marked the same, with the exception of the catalog number which is "Cat 157T26" and "A General Electric Organization." $45.00 ea.

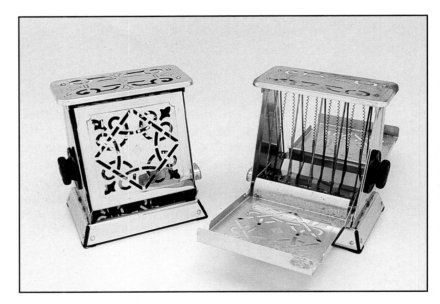

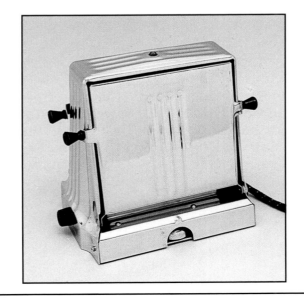

HOTPOINT

mid 1930s, 6¼" high, chrome plated body with black Bakelite handles and knobs, light and dark heat control. One door is marked on top edge: "Use This Side For One Slice." This door also has a cut-out arrow on top edge. The heat signal light on top of the toaster, as well as the bell on the bottom of the toaster, lets you know when the toast is ready to be turned, which is done by lowering the doors which turns the toast and toasting resumes. Marked on the bottom: "General Electric Cat No129T42 Hotpoint. Volts 115 Watts 500 Patents 1481.021 1540628 and Pending. General Electric Co. Bridgeport Conn. USA Ontario Calif. For Alternating Current." $55.00.

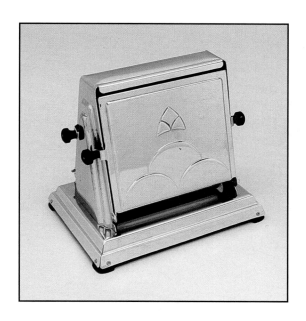

HOTPOINT

mid 1930s, 7⅛" high, chrome plated body with black Bakelite handles and wafer feet, mica heating elements, no heat control. Marked on the bottom: "General GE Electric Cat No. 119T38 Hotpoint, Volts 115 Watts 470 General Electric Co. Bridgeport Conn. USA Ontario Calif." $35.00.

JUSTRITE

1930s, 6⅝" high, nickel plated body with wafer door pulls, mica heating element, no heat control. Marked on the bottom: "Cat. No. JT-1111 Volts 110-120 Watts 530 Justrite Elec. & Mfg. Co. Minneapolis, Minn." $45.00.

THE K-M COMPANY

Reverso, 1930s, 6¾" high, chrome plated body with painted black enamel base, fancy fiber handles. Wire coil heating element is laced through ceramic hook style fasteners. No heat control. Marked on the bottom: "115V Pat. Nos. 80-348 1,756,784, 500W K.M. Reverso Reg. US Pat. Off. The K-M Company Belleville, Ill. Cat. No. 510 USA." Note: K-M Company stands for Knapp Monarch. $50.00.

THE K-M COMPANY

KM Reverso, 1930s, 6¾" high, nickel plated body with black painted base, wafer style handles, no heat control, vertically laced open spring coil heating element. Marked on the bottom: "110 V Patent Nos. 80,348 1,756,784 500W KM Reverso Reg. US Pat. Off. The K-M Company Belleville Ill. USA." $40.00.

THE K-M COMPANY

Knapp-Monarch, late 1930s, 7" high chrome plated body with wooden handles and black painted base. Marked on bottom: "K-M Reg US Pat. Off. 115V 800W Pats Pend The K-M Company St. Louis MO. USA Cat. No. 525." This toaster has no heat control, and the toast has to be popped up manually. The laced coil heating elements toast the bread on both sides at once. $125.00.

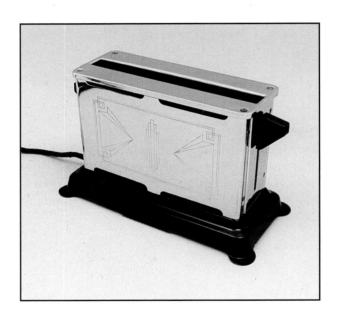

THE K-M COMPANY

late 1930s – 1940s, 7¾" high, chrome plated body with brown Bakelite handles and feet. Paper label reads: "K.M. Knapp Monarch Co. Electrical Servants Cat. No. 21-501 400 Watts 115V Pat. Nos. 1,756,784 - 2,266,324 Knapp Monarch Co. St. Louis USA." Note: When handle on the right side of toaster is turned toward you, it opens the door out toward you, and when the handle is turned away from you, it opens the door on the other side. The handle on the left is stationary. Bread has to be turned manually. $45.00.

THE K-M COMPANY

1940s, 7⅞" high, chrome plated body with brown Bakelite handles and feet. Label reads: "K.M. Knapp Monarch, St. Louis USA Cat. No. 21-502 149 400W 115V Pat # 1,756,784 - 2,206,324. 250." Each door is operated manually and separately. When handle on right is turned down toward you, it opens the front door. When the handle is turned down and away from you, it opens the back door. Left side handle is stationary. $35.00.

KENMORE

late 1930s, 7⅛" high, chrome body with black wooden handles and feet, mica heating element, no heat control. Marked on the bottom: "Kenmore. Sears, Roebuck & Co. Volts 110-120 Watts 450 Amps 3.91 Model No. 307,6322 H-8." $40.00.

KENMORE

1940s, 7½" high, chrome plated body with Bakelite handles and knobs, light and dark heat control. Marked on the bottom: "Kenmore Sears, Roebuck & Co. Volts 110-120 Watts 660 Amps 5.74 Model No. 3076329 AC Only H-8." $50.00.

TOASTERS

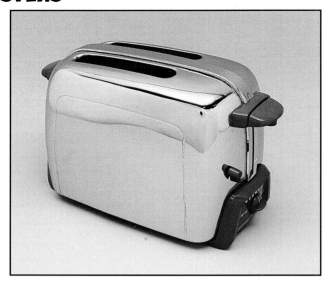

KENMORE*
late 1940s, 7⅝" high, chrome body with green Bakelite handles and feet. The marking on the bottom is the same as the one pictured at the bottom of the page with the exception of the serial which is 63. All are marked UL. I have been told that there was a blue version produced as well. The blue is supposedly the easiest to find, but I have yet to see one. $145.00.

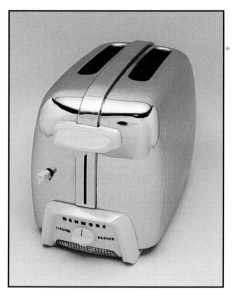

KENMORE*
late 1940s, 7⅝" high, chrome body with yellow Bakelite handles and feet. The marking on the bottom is the same as toaster below with the exception of the model and serial number, model 344-63321, and serial number 83. $145.00.

KENMORE*
late 1940s, 7⅝" high, chrome body with red Bakelite handles and feet. Marked on the bottom: "Kenmore Our Own Trademark For Sears, Roebuck Co Model 344-6332 Automatic Pop-up Toaster Operates On AC Only Serial Number 152 Volts 110-120 Amps 10.4 Watts 1200." (10 patents listed on bottom, and other pats pend.) $145.00. Note: Kenmore is a Sears Roebuck Company trade name.

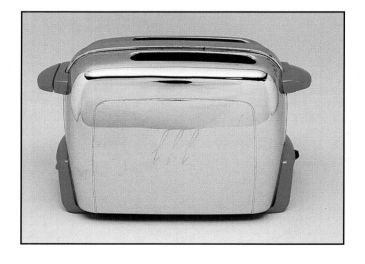

*Toasters manufactured by Arvin Noblitt – Sparks Industries for Sears Roebuck Co.

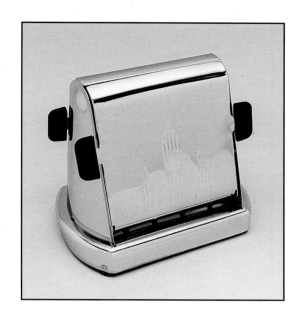

KENMORE

1950s, 7¼" high, chrome plated body with Bakelite handles and wafer feet. Marked on the bottom: "Renfrew Electric and Refrigerator Co. Ltd. Renfrew Canada Cat. No. 451 Volts 120 Watts 450 AC Only CSA App. No. 103 Patented 1951 Made In Canada." $45.00.

KENMORE

same as pictured above, shown in open position. Note: The double door connecting rod on each side is applied towards the upper and lower section of the toaster body. When manually operated, these rods swing the door up, over, and out in a downward position. Toast is then turned over or removed with less chance of burning your fingers. Unique mechanism. $45.00.

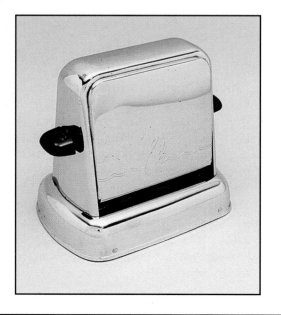

KWIKWAY

1930s, 7⅜" high, chrome body with brown Bakelite handles, mica heating element, no heat control. Doors are operated simultaneously when handle on right is turned downward. Marked on the bottom: "Kwikway Reg. US Pat. Off. Kwikway Co. St. Louis USA 115V 400W Cat No-21-404 Pat. No. 5 (other patent numbers listed) and Pats. Pend." $40.00.

KWIKWAY

mid 1930s, 7⅛" high, chrome body with black wooden door pulls, vertical laced open spring-coil heating element. No heat control. Marked on the bottom: Cat. No. K-55 Pat. Nos. 80,348 - 1,756,784. Series A 115V 450W Reg. US Pat. Off. Kwikway Toaster. Kwikway Co. St. Louis, Mo." $40.00.

L&H ELECTRICS

late 1920s, 7¼" high, nickel plated body with black handles and fiber feet, no heat control. Marked on the upper front side of the base: "L&H Electrics Trademark Model 204 Volts 110-120 Watts 550 A.J. Lindemann & Hoverson Co. Milwaukee, Wis, USA (5 patent numbers listed)." $30.00.

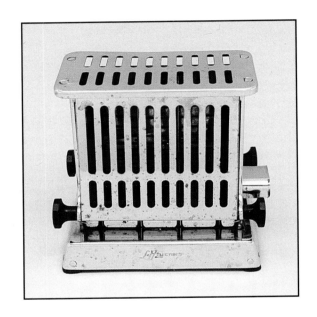

L&H AUTOMATIC

1930s, 8¼" high, chrome body. Marked on the bottom: "L&H Electrics. Automatic Toaster Model 205 Watts 660 Volts 110-120. Patents Pending A.J. Lindemann & Hoverson Co. Milwaukee, Wis. Made in USA." This toaster toasts two slices of bread when the door on top is pulled open, which also closes the bottom slots where the bread rests. Bread is placed in the toaster, timer is set; when browning is complete, the bottom slots open and the toast drops down and out of each side. This toaster also has an off-on switch, and a lift lever that is used manually to open the bottom doors to release the toast. $250.00.

L&H TURNS IT

1924 – 1930, 7⅜" high, nickel plated body, black Bakelite door pulls. Nameplate reads: "L&H Turns it Toaster Volts 110-120 Watts 500 Mod 202 AJ Lindemann & Hoverson Co. Milwaukee, Wis. USA." Note: The lower inside section of the door has a plate attached to it, and when the door is pulled down, it pushes the bread out on the door for turning. This device was patented by Edwin Rutenber while working for the Lindemann & Hoverson Co. Also note the oval-shaped top design to keep the toast or a coffee pot warm until needed. The coffee pot shown is Granite Ware, and the color is referred to as Chrysolite. $45.00 toaster.

LANDERS, FRARY, & CLARK

late 1920s, 7⅞" high, chrome body. Name tag reads: "Landers, Made in USA Landers, Frary & Clark. New Britain Conn. No. E 7542 Volts 108/116 Watts 550 Pat. Applied For." Note: By pushing the long lever, and letting it snap back against the small open lever, the door comes out to place bread in toast basket; the toast basket is then pushed back into the toaster manually. Bread is toasted on both sides at once. Round lever is set for desired brownness. When you push the long lever down to the top of the browning lever, the timer begins and when toast is done, the long lever comes up and pushes the open button. The door then pops out automatically and toaster shuts off. $85.00.

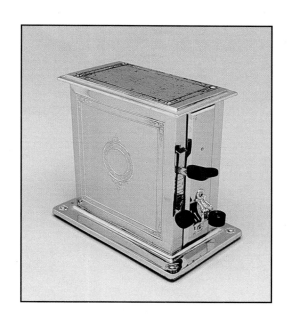

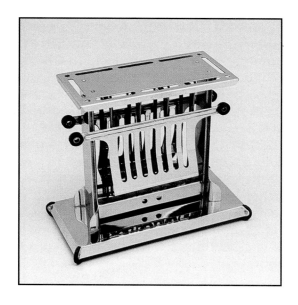

LANDERS, FRARY, & CLARK

Thermax, 1920s, 6¾" high, nickel plated body with fiber handles and feet, laced open spring-coil heating element. Bottom nameplate reads: "Thermax Volt 108-116 No. E3946 Watts 500 Landers, Frary & Clark. New Britain Conn USA Made in USA Pat. Applied For." $55.00.

LANDERS, FRARY, & CLARK

Thermax, 1920s, 7¼" high, nickel plated body with black handles and feet, no heat control. Marked on the bottom: "Thermax Made By Landers, Frary & Clark. New Britain Conn USA Volts 108/116 Number E3412 Watts 625 Made in USA Pat. July 28, 1914." Note: This type toaster is referred to as a "turn-easy." $40.00.

LANDERS, FRARY, & CLARK

Thermax, 1915 – 1920s, 6⅝" high, nickel plated body with black base, wafer handles and feet, 3 section horizontal mica heating element. Nameplate on bottom reads: "Thermax Landers, Frary & Clark. New Britain Conn, USA, Volts 115/120 No. E 3941 Amps 2.9 Patents LMP Pending." $40.00.

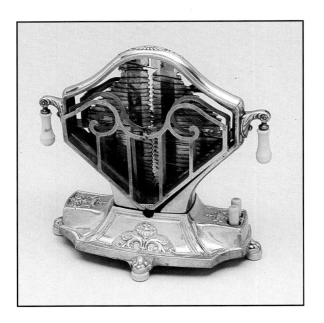

LANDERS, FRARY, & CLARK

Universal E9410, 1929, 8¼" high, nickel plated fancy embossed body. Nameplate on bottom reads: "The Trademark Known In Every Home. Universal 117/125 No E9410 Watts 125 Landers, Frary & Clark. New Britain Conn. USA." In May of 1929 the design patent on the styling of the ultimate swinger was granted to George Curtiss for the unique heart-shaped design with beautiful fancy embossed body and tear-drop handles. Warner and Lamb had created a push-button masterpiece that was never patented. The working order of the toast baskets is fascinating, each basket is controlled by its own push-button. When button is pushed, basket turns half cycle and stops for bread to be placed in the basket; push button again and the cycle is complete with the bread against the heating element. When the button is pushed again, the cycle is completed in reverse for toasting the other side. Special note: The 1929 Autumn and Christmas trade were very fortunate to purchase such a toaster masterpiece. $800.00.

LANDERS, FRARY, & CLARK

Universal Double-Quick Oven Toaster, 1930s, 6⅝" high, gleaming chromium with black Bakelite handles and fiber feet. Bottom nameplate reads: "The Trademark Known In Every Home, Universal. Made By Landers, Frary & Clark. New Britain Conn. USA No. E 7722C Volts 108/116 Watts 660." The toast rack tilts forward at the touch of a finger, takes bread up to 4" x 4¾". Note: A toaster like this one was pictured in a November 1937 reprinted catalog of the Universal Electric Appliances. $65.00.

LANDERS, FRARY, & CLARK

Universal E944, 1920s, 6⅝" high, nickel plated body with wafer handles and black wooden knob and feet, 3-part horizontal mica heating element patented by Warner in 1913. The fancy pierced frame is the art of George Curtiss who was granted a design patent for it. Marked on the attached stamped sheet steel base weight: "Universal Made By Landers, Frary & Clark. New Britain Conn. USA Volts 110 No. E944 Amps 3.1 Lmp Pat. Feb. 6, 1906 Patents Dec. 9, 1913 Oct. 5, 1915 Great Britain 15961-1912, 22258-1912 Canada June 1, 1915 BTE SG DUG No. 44654B." $65.00.

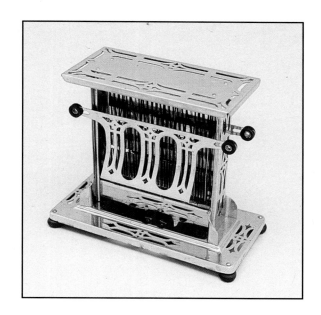

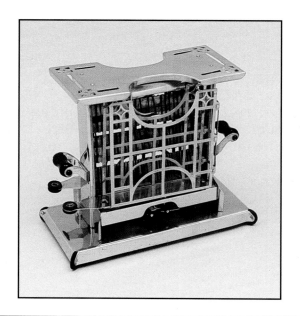

LANDERS, FRARY, & CLARK

Universal E947, 1920s, same as toaster at top of following page except this style has the wooden carrying handles on the side. $75.00.

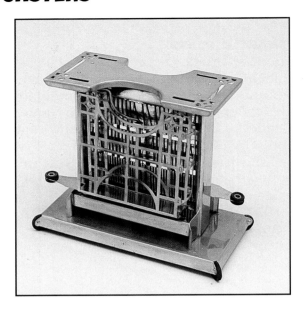

LANDERS, FRARY, & CLARK

Universal E947, 1920, 6⅝" high, nickel plated body with fiber handles and feet, 3-part horizontal mica heating element. Marked on the attached base: "Weights stamped from Heavy Sheet Steel, Patents Dec. 9, 1913 Oct. 5, 1913 Great Britain 15961-1912, 22258-1912 Canada June 1, 1915 BTE SG DUG No. 446548 Universal Made By Landers, Frary & Clark. New Britain Conn, USA Volts 106-114 No. E947 Amps 3.6 Lmp Pat. Feb. 6, 1906 Patents Nov. 16, 1920 Pat. Feb 6, 1906 Patents Pending." $55.00.

LANDERS, FRARY, & CLARK

Universal E947, 1920s, same as top photo except this one has the laced coil heating element. $75.00.

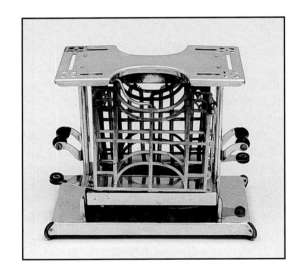

LANDERS, FRARY, & CLARK

Universal E949X, 1920s, 7¼" high, nickel plated body with fiber door handles and wooden carrying handles and feet, laced coil heating element. Note: This toaster is the largest of the four shown, and the base design is also different. $95.00.

LANDERS, FRARY, & CLARK

Universal, 1906 – 1920s, 6¾" high, nickel plated body with fiber handles and feet, 3-part horizontal mica heating element. Marked on the attached stamped sheet steel base weight: "Patents Dec. 9, 1913 Oct. 5, 1915 Great Britain 15961-1912, 22258 1912. Canada June 1, 1915 BTE SG DUG No. 446548 Univeral. Made By Landers, Frary & Clark. New Britain Conn. USA Volts 106-114 No. E946 Amps 3.1 Lmp Pat. Feb. 6, 1906 Feb. 6, 1908. (other patents listed.) Patents Pending." $55.00.

LANDERS, FRARY, & CLARK

Universal, 1930s, 6⅝" high, chrome body with black handles, mica heating element. Marked on the bottom: "Universal Made By Landers, Frary & Clark. New Britain Conn. USA Volts108/116 No. E7312 Watts 625 Made in the USA Pat. July 28, 1914." $35.00.

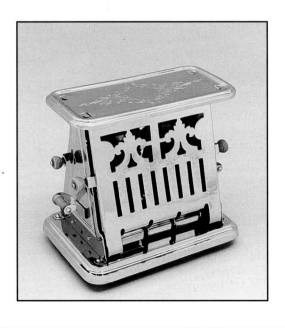

LANDERS, FRARY, & CLARK

Universal, 1914, 7¼" high, metal plated with durable non-tarnish chromium, ivory casium knobs, carrying handles and feet. Nameplate reads: "The Trademark Known In Every Home Universal Volts 108-116 No. E7812 Watts 625 Landers, Frary & Clark. New Britain Conn. USA Pat. July 28, 1914." $55.00.

LANDERS, FRARY, & CLARK

Universal, 1920s, 6⅝" high, chrome body with black insulating wafer handles and feet. The heating element is a vertically laced open spring-coil. This toaster has no heat control. Nameplate reads "Universal. The Trademark Known In Every Home. Volts 108/116 No. E946 Watts 500, Landers, Frary & Clark. New Britain Conn. USA." Note: This toaster has never been used. $55.00 w/cord.

LANDERS, FRARY, & CLARK

Universal, 1920s, 7¼" high, chrome body with black wooden door pulls and feet, mica heating element, no heat control. Marked on the bottom: "The Trademark Known In Every Home: Universal. Made In USA Landers, Frary & Clark. New Britain Conn. USA No. E79312 Volts 110/120 Watts 625." $50.00.

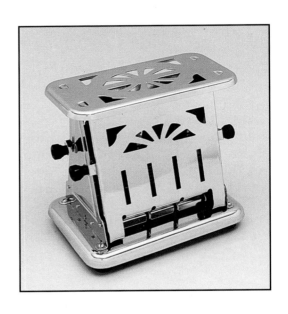

LANDERS, FRARY, & CLARK

Universal, 1925, 6⅞" high including toast rack, nickel plated body with black wooden handles, knob, and feet, no heat control. Bottom nameplate reads: "Universal Landers, Frary & Clark. New Britain Conn. USA Volts 106-114 No. E942 Amps 5 Patents Pending." Note: Toast rack door is pulled out and bread is inserted in the rack and pushed back in the toaster where it is toasted on both sides at once. Door is pulled out manually to check if toast is done. Toaster has to be unplugged to shut it off. $55.00.

LANDERS, FRARY, & CLARK

Universal, 1930s, 7¼" high, chrome body with black Bakelite door pulls and feet, mica heating element, no heat control. Marked on the bottom: "The Trademark Known In Every Home. Universal Made In USA Landers, Frary & Clark. New Britain Conn. USA No. E7912A Volts 110-120 Watts 625." $35.00.

LANDERS, FRARY, & CLARK

Universal, 1930s, 7¼" high, chrome plated body with black wooden handles and feet, mica heating element. Marked on the bottom: "Universal Made By Landers, Frary & Clark. New Britain Conn. USA Volts 110/120 No. E7211. Made In USA Pat." $35.00.

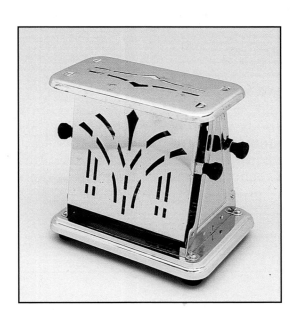

LANDERS, FRARY, & CLARK

Universal, 1940s, 7⅝" high, chrome plated body with brown Bakelite handles, knobs, and base, light and dark heat control knob. Marked on the bottom: "Universal Manufactured By Landers, Frary & Clark. New Britain Conn, Pat. No. 2,361,078 Volts 110-120 No. EA B2601 Watts 150 Made in USA." Note: When the middle knob is pushed down, it turns the toaster on, and when the toast is done, the handle is pushed down which then pops the toast up and turns the toaster off. $35.00.

LANDERS, FRARY, & CLARK

Universal, early 1900s, 7¼" high, chrome plated body with Bakelite handles and feet. Nameplate on bottom reads: "The Trademark Known In Every Home, Universal Made In USA. Landers, Frary & Clark. New Britain Conn. USA No. E 7812 Volts 110/120 Watts 625." $50.00.

LANDERS, FRARY, & CLARK

Universal E944, 1920s, 6⅝" high, nickel plated body with wafer handles and feet, laced open spring-coil heating element. Bottom nameplate reads: "The Trademark Known In Every Home, Universal. Volts 108-116 No. E944 Watts 500 Made in USA Landers, Frary & Clark. New Britain Conn. USA." $65.00.

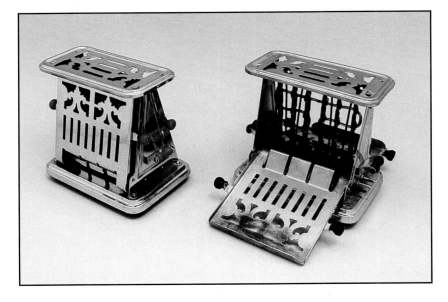

Left:
LANDERS, FRARY, & CLARK

Universal, approximately 1912, 7¼" high, chrome body with red Bakelite knobs and carrying handles and black feet. Nameplate reads: "The Trademark Known In Every Home Universal, Volts 108-116 No. E95412 Watts 625 Made in USA, Landers, Frary & Clark. New Britain Conn. USA. Patent Applied For." The heating element for this toaster is advertised in an old Universal catalog as long-life Nichrome wire wound on thick mica cores. This assures fast and even toasting. $45.00.

Right:
LANDERS, FRARY, & CLARK

Universal, approximately 1912, 7¼" high, chrome body with black wooden carrying handles and knobs. Nameplate reads the same with the exception of the model number which is E9412. This toaster has a horizontal laced wire coil heating element. $45.00.

LANDERS, FRARY, & CLARK
Universal, 1918 – 1923, with attached toast warming rack, 6⅝" high without rack, 10⅛" with rack, highly polished nickel body with a Joseph Lamb base. The attached 1913 Thermax weight base is marked "Pat. Dec. 9, 13 Oct. 5, 15 GT BTN Made By Landers, Frary & Clark. New Britain Conn." Note: The Warner patented heating elements are three horizontal sections of mica wrapped with wire, the riveted feet are insulated fiber wafers. $140.00.

LANDERS, FRARY, & CLARK
Universal, late 1920s, 7⅛" high, chrome doors and sides with black painted top and base, black wooden door pulls and feet, mica heating element, no heat control. Nameplate on bottom reads: "The Trademark Known In Every Home, Universal Made in USA Landers, Frary & Clark. New Britain Conn. USA No. E3612 Volts 110-120. Watts 626." $35.00.

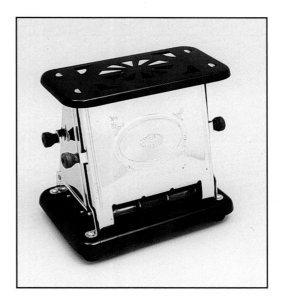

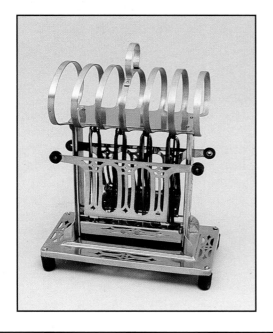

LANDERS, FRARY, & CLARK
Universal, 1920s, with attached toast warming rack, 7¼" without toast rack, 10¾" with toast warming rack, polished nickel body. Attached base weight marked: "Universal Made By Landers, Frary & Clark. New Britain Conn, USA Volts 106/114 No. E945 Amps 4.5 Patents Dec. 9, 1913 Oct. 5, 1915 Great Britain 15961-1912, 22258-1912 Canada June 1, 1915 BTESG DUG No. 446548 Patents Pending Nov. 16, 1920 Feb. 14, 1922 Jan. 31, 1922 Feb. 6, 1906." The heating element is an open lace spring-coil element. The feet are wood. George Curtiss was granted the patent for the extraordinary pierced body. This toaster is referred to as a "pincher." Price with toast warming rack $155.00.

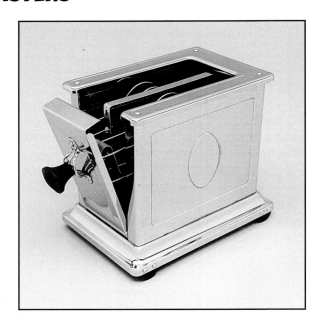

LANDERS, FRARY, & CLARK
Universal Double-Quick Oven, late 1930s, 6⅝" high, gleaming chromium with black Bakelite handles, fiber feet that protect the tabletop's surface. Marked on the bottom: "Universal Made By Landers, Frary & Clark. New Britain Conn. Volts 110/120 No. E7722F Watts 800 Made In USA." This toaster has the knobs lower down on the doors and side; the one pictured on page 55 has the knobs near the top edge of the toaster. The brackets that hold the knobs are secured in an up and down position; the knobs on the other toaster are secured in a side-ways manner. $65.00.

LANDERS, FRARY, & CLARK
Universal, late 1930s, 7¼" high, chrome plated body with brown Bakelite handles and attached side feet. Bottom marked: "Universal Made By Landers, Frary & Clark. New Britain Conn. USA Volts 110/120 No. E 1221A Watts 525 Pat. Made in USA." $35.00.

LANDERS, FRARY, & CLARK
Universal, Muffin and Bread, 1930s, Devonshire pattern, 7¼" high, chromium plated, mahogany composition trim. Toasts bread 5" x 4¾". Its specially designed bread rack also holds muffins. Marked on the bottom: "Universal Made By Landers, Frary & Clark. New Britain Conn. Volts 110/120 No. E221 Watts 525 Made in USA Pat. 2172687." $60.00.

LANDERS, FRARY, & CLARK

Universal, 1940s, 7½" high, chrome plated body with black Bakelite handles, knobs, and base, light and dark heat control. Marked on top edge: "Universal." Marked on the bottom: "Universal Manufactured By Landers, Frary & Clark. New Britain Conn. Pat. No. 236, 107C Volts 110-120 No. EA2815 Watts 1150 Made in the USA." Note: This toaster has a special built-in feature called SER-VUE; you can remove one slice while the other continues to toast. "No need to eat cold toast or waste bread, toast can automatically be re-warmed in seconds to appetizing crispness without burning." $40.00.

LANDERS, FRARY, & CLARK

Universal, 1940s, 7⅝" high, chromium plated body with brown Bakelite handles and base, mica heating element, no heat control. The handle on the right side has a dual opening flip-over action. The handle on the left side is stationary. Marked on the bottom: "Universal Landers, Frary & Clark. New Britain Conn. Made In USA Volts 110-120 Watts 500 Article No. EA 2105." Note: The aerodynamically shaped body. $55.00.

LASCO

Automatic Pop-Up, 1940s, 7½" high. 115 volts AC/DC model No. 8. 550 watts, mfg. by Lasco Metal Products Inc. Westchester Pa. Pat. pending 730385, made in U.S.A. Note: The unique styling of this toaster. $125.00.

LEDIG

Toaster-Cooker, early 1920s, 7¼" high, nickel plated body. Bottom nameplate reads: "110 Volts 600 Watts, Pat. Aug. 19, 1921 Other Patents Pending Pat'd. Lmp Feb. 6, 06 Ledig Toaster-Cooker, No. 500 A. Mecky Co. Philadelphia." Note: This spherical-shaped toaster is very unique; it comes with a toast basket (not shown), a sandwich holder, and a pan for melting butter. Each piece is slid sideways into the toaster, one at a time. The attached top toast rack helps to keep the upper section of the toaster together as well as keeping the toast warm. The inner sides of the toaster act as reflectors to reflect heat toward the bread for toasting. $650.00 without toast basket. $750.00 with toast basket.

LEXINGTON MACHINERY DEVELOPMENT CO. INC.

Toast Queen, 1930s, 6¾" high, chrome body with black Bakelite handles, wooden feet, no heat control. Marked on bottom: "Toast Queen Lexington Machinery Development Co. Inc. Clifton N.J. 115V 500-650W." $35.00.

MADE-RITE
late 1920s, 7⅞" high, nickel plated body with wood handles, no heat control. Marked on the bottom: "Made-Rite Mfg. Co. Sandusky. O. Made-Rite 500W 110V Cat A 820." The pattern on the doors resembles the Marion Giant Flip Flop #66. $35.00.

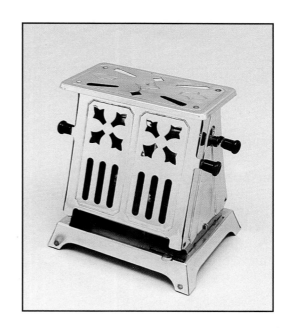

MADE-RITE
1930s, 7⅞" high, nickel plated with black Bakelite handles. Marked on the bottom: "Made-Rite, Made-Rite Mfg. Co. Sandusky, O. 525W 110V Cat. A842." $65.00.

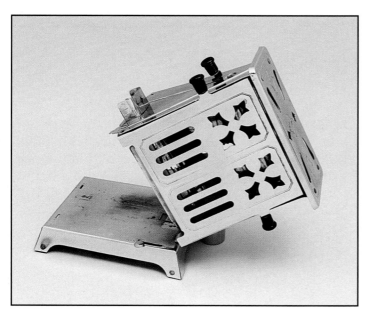

MADE-RITE
this view shows how the toaster above can be tipped up or removed from the base by pushing the open and lock lever to the open position. Pushing the lever back to the right locks the body to the base. This unique design permits easy access to the crumb section for cleaning. $65.00.

MAJESTIC ELECTRIC APPLIANCE CO.
1930s, 7⅜" high, chrome plated doors and top with black enamel painted base, black Bakelite handles and black concealed wafer style feet, mica heating element, no heat control. Marked on the bottom: "Majestic Volts 110-120 Style No. 462 Watts 550 Manufactured By Majestic Electric Appliance Co. Minneapolis-San Francisco." $95.00.

MALDA ELECTRIC MFG. CO.
1930s, 6⅝" high, chrome body with black wafer door pulls and feet, mica heating element, no heat control. Marked on the bottom: "Malda Model No. 84 115V 550W Malda Elec. Mfg. Co. Chicago." $45.00.

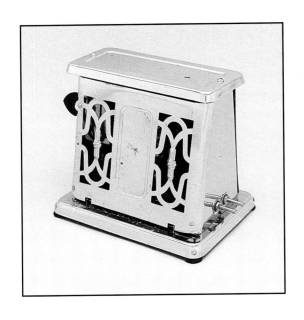

MALDA ELECTRIC MFG. CO.
late 1900s, 7" high, chrome body with black Bakelite handles on one side of each door, wafer feet, no heat controls. Marked on bottom: "Malda Model No. 74 115 Volts 550W Malda Elec. Mfg. Co. Chicago." $45.00.

MANNING-BOWMAN & CO.
Automatic Pop-up, 1950s, 6⅜" high, chrome plated body with black handles, knobs, and feet. Marked on the bottom: "Manning Bowman Automatic Pop-up Toaster Model No. 34502 Operates On AC Only. 115 Volts 740 Watts. Manning Bowman Division McGraw-Edison Company Boonville, Missouri." $25.00.

MANNING-BOWMAN & CO.
1930s, 7½" high, chrome body with black Bakelite carrying handles and timer knob, light and dark heat control, removable crumb tray. Marked on the bottom: "Manning-Bowman Volts 110-125 Watts 680 Serial No. 7-33 Article No. K-105 Manning Bowman & Co. Meriden, Conn." Note: Light and dark heat control is set by pushing down black timer knob on the side. When bread is toasted to the desired brownness, the toaster shuts off automatically then toast is manually released out the side. $125.00.

MANNING-BOWMAN & CO.
1920s, 7¼" high, nickel plated, fancy embossed body with black Bakelite knobs and feet. Marked on the bottom: "M.B. Means Best", Serial No. 4-26 Article No. 1229 Manning Bowman & Co Meriden Conn. Made in USA Volts 106-115 Watts 600 Patents Pending." Open spring-coil heating element is laced over a ceramic core rod designed especially to hold the elements apart. $60.00.

MANNING-BOWMAN & CO.

1930s, 7½" high, chrome body with black wooden handles, light and dark heat control, side pull-out crumb tray. Marked on the bottom: "Made By Manning Bowman & Co. Meriden, Conn. USA. Volts 110-120 Watts 650 Cat No. 108 Serial No. 8-37 Pat No. 97659." When toast is done, toaster shuts off automatically, and the side door stays closed in its located position until it is manually pulled open and toast drops out on the door. The door does not drop down very far because there are no sides to hold the toast from dropping sideways out the door. $65.00.

MANNING-BOWMAN & CO.

late 1920s – early 1930s, 7¼" high, chrome plated body with black Bakelite handles and wafer feet, no heat control. Marked on the bottom: "Made By Manning Bowman & Co Meriden, Conn USA Volts 110-125 Watts 550 Cat. No. K639 Serial No. 4-34." $60.00.

MANNING-BOWMAN & CO.

1930s, 7¼" high, Aranium plate. Marked on the bottom: "Serial No. 2-28 M.B. Means Best Article No. 1228 Manning-Bowman & Co. Meriden Conn, Made in USA. Volts 110-115 Watts 600 Patented Oct. 12, 1926." $45.00.

MANNING-BOWMAN & CO.
mid 1930s, 7½" high, brilliant chromium with walnut handles and feet. Marked on the bottom: "Made By Manning-Bowman & Co. Meriden Conn. USA Volts 110-120 Watts 470 Cat. No. 83 Serial No. 7-36." This model is named "The Puritan." $40.00.

MANNING-BOWMAN & CO.
mid 1930s, 7½" high, non-tarnishing chromium with black heat-resisting molded knobs and feet. Marked on the bottom: "Made By The Manning-Bowman & Co. Meriden Conn. USA Volts 110-120 Watts 470 Cat. No. 78 Serial No." Note: Advertised in the Manning-Bowman catalog as "THE SKYLINE, it toasts two full-size slices of bread at once in speedy time due to the heat conserving all metal doors. To automatically turn bread for toasting simply lower the door." $40.00.

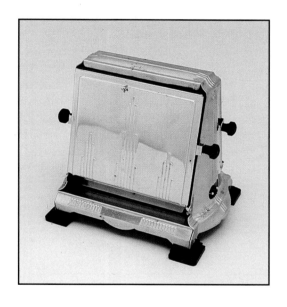

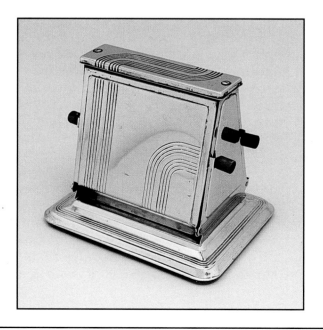

MANNING-BOWMAN & CO.
mid 1930s, 7" high, chromium finish with solid walnut handles. Marked on the bottom: "Made By Manning Bowman & Co. Meriden Conn. USA, Volts 110-120 Watts 470 Cat. No. 82 Serial No. 6-37." Note: Manning-Bowman 1937 catalog advertises this model as "The Pioneer, Doors Are Of Solid Metal That Can Conserve The Heat." The heating unit is the speedy nichrome-wound mica type. $30.00.

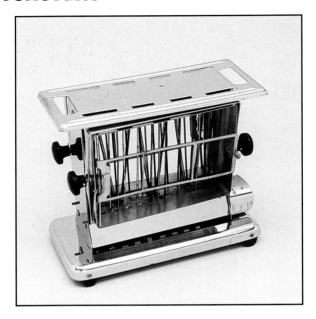

MANNING-BOWMAN & CO.

Reversible, early 1900s, 6¼" high, nickel plated body with black wooden handles. Marked on the bottom: "Manning Bowman Quality. Volts 110 Amps 4 Serial No-Article No. 1215, Meriden Conn. USA Lmp Pat. Feb. 6, 06." Laced open spring-coil heating element. Each of the open style toast doors is marked on the top and bottom "Reversible Toaster." $125.00.

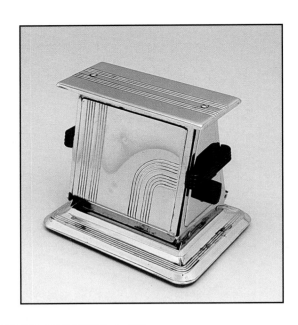

MANNING-BOWMAN & CO.

late 1930s, 6¾" high, chrome plated body with brown Bakelite handles. Marked on bottom: "Made By Manning-Bowman & Co. Meriden Conn. USA Volts 110-120 Watts 420 Cat. No. 85 Serial No. 11-38." Note: The knob on the right side of toaster opens and closes both doors one quarter of the way simultaneously. There is a wire attached to the inner lower section of the doors to keep bread pushed against each door. Due to the design of the doors opening only a quarter of the way, I believe there were a lot of burned fingers when removing or turning toast. $45.00.

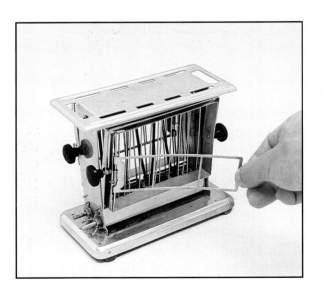

MANNING-BOWMAN & CO.

Reversible, early 1900s, 6¼" high, nickel plated body with black wooden handles. Marked on the bottom: "Manning Bowman Quality. Volts 110 Amps 4 Serial No. 78337 Article No. 1215. Meriden Conn. USA Pat Feb. 2, 1915 Patents Pending." There are considerable differences on the bottom markings of this toaster compared to the above left toaster. The heating elements have also been applied differently. The plug prongs on the above toaster are flat and covered, whereas this toaster has rounded exposed prongs. Note: This photo shows how the bread is placed in the baskets by pulling out the small spring-loaded door on the front of the basket. After the first side is browned, the door is reversed manually for toasting on the other side. When toasting is done, the small door must be opened manually, probably by using a fork since this door will be very hot, and there is a very small loop that a prong of a fork would fit into. There is only a spring-loaded small door on one side of each toast basket. $125.00.

MANNING-BOWMAN & CO.

Reversible, 1920s, 7⅜" high, highly polished nickel body. Nameplate reads: "Serial No. 9-25 MB Means Best. Article No. 1225 Volts 110 Watts 600 Manning Bowman & Co. Meriden Conn. Lmp Pat. Feb. 6,06. Made in USA." $125.00.

MANNING-BOWMAN & CO.

Reversible, same toaster as pictured above but in open position. Each toast basket has two attached wire doors. When these doors are pulled out manually, the bread can be placed in for toasting. The center wire on these doors has a bend in it for your finger to grab. The door is flipped over to toast the other side by turning the black knob. Top of doors are marked: "Patented Dec. 4TH, 1923. Reversible Toaster. Pat. Dec. 28, 1920." $125.00.

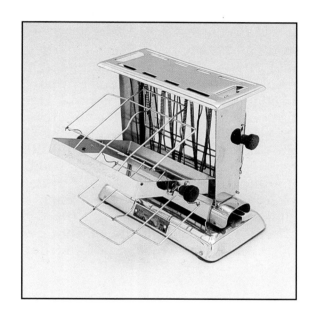

MANNING-BOWMAN & CO.

Homelectric, late 1920s – early 1930s, 7¼" high, chromium plated body with black Bakelite handles and wafer feet, mica heating elements. Marked on the bottom: "Made By Manning-Bowman & Co. Volts 110-125 Watts 550 Cat No. K63 Serial No.____." $45.00.

MASTERCRAFT FULL VISION

1930s, 7" high, chrome body with four full vision windows, black painted base and wooden handles, no heat control, laced spring-coil heating element. Nameplate on bottom reads: "Mastercraft Full Vision Electric Toaster Cat. No. 2009. 115V 450W Pat. Nos. 99,287. 1,756,784. 2,029,575. Pats. Pend." This toaster is one of my favorites. When the bread is being toasted, this toaster gives off a warm glow through the four, full vision windows, giving you a warm feeling to start off your day. $100.00.

MASTERCRAFT

mid 1930s, 6¾" high, nickel plated doors, black painted base and top, wooden door pulls, mica heating element, no heat control. Marked on the bottom: "Mastercraft BMC Model No. 85 Watts 520 Volts 115." Note: There is a single door pull on each side. The doors of this toaster have been painted with an aluminum paint, not by the manufacturer. The doors are attached to the base with one cotter key on each side that is slipped through an eyelet on the base. A small spring is attached at the bottom center of the door and base which holds the doors closed. $35.00.

MERIDEN HOMELECTRIC

mid 1920s, 7¼" high, body is highly polished nickel plate with black wooden door knobs and wafer feet. Marked on the bottom: "Meriden Homelectric Manning-Bowman & Co. Meriden Conn. USA Volts-106-115 Watts 600 Cat. No.60 Serial No. 11-27." The coil heating element is laced eight times from top to bottom. Element is held in place by wire type hooks. The plug prongs are flat style. Both doors are held shut by a spring in the bottom center of the door. Each door is operated manually. Bread has to be turned manually. This type toaster is called a "pincher." $55.00.

MERIT MADE
late 1930s, 8¼" high, chrome body with applied aluminum finish over the chrome, black Bakelite handles. Marked on the bottom: "Merit Made Inc. Model Z 375 Watts 115 Volts Serial No." Buffalo, N.Y. Made In USA. Pat. App. For." When the lever on top is *pushed down*, both doors open simultaneously. Note: Other styles of this toaster are shown in the book. The reason we have shown this one is the shape of the base. $95.00.

MERIT MADE
late 1930s, 8¼" high, chrome body with doors that have an applied aluminum finish and black painted base. This toaster has the same marking on the bottom as the toaster below except the number stamped is 029046. $75.00.

MERIT MADE
late 1930s, 8¼" high, metal body with applied aluminum finish, black painted base molded metal feet, black Bakelite handles and knob, mica heating element, no heat control. Marked on the bottom: "Merit Made Inc. Model-Z 375 Watts 115 Volts. Serial No.____ Buffalo, N.Y. Made in USA Pat. App. For." (Part of a number is stamped on the bottom.) When the lever on top is *pulled up*, both doors open simultaneously. $95.00.

MERIT

1940s, 8¼" high, chrome body with Bakelite handles. Marked: "Merit Made Inc., Model A 800 Watts 115 Volts AC Only Serial No. _____ Buffalo N.Y. Made in USA Pat. Appl. For." No heat control light. Note: All three toasters have a pull-out crumb tray marked "Crumb Tray." $100.00.

MERIT

1940s, 8" high, chrome body with Bakelite handles, red heat control light. Marked: "Merit Made Inc. Model 800 Watts 115 Volts Serial No. _____ Buffalo N.Y. Made In The USA Patent Applied For." On the reverse side of the toaster is embossed the letter "M" in a circle, which stands for Merit. Also on the back lower section is a button for dark, medium, and light settings. On the lower left side there is a release lever that pops up toast. The red heat control light lets you know when the toaster is operating and when it shuts off. $150.00.

MIRACLE ELECTRIC CO.

late 1930s, body has a "baked-on" enamel finish of a dark, steel grayish-brown, black painted base with Bakelite handles and feet, no heat control. Side of base marked "Miracle." Bottom marked: "Miracle Electric Co. Chicago 3, Illinois Patent No. D101359 Cat. No. 210-115V-400 Watts Made In USA." $35.00.

MERIT

Note: This toaster is the same as the photo above with the exception there is no red heat control light. $100.00.

MONTGOMERY WARD

1930s, 7⅛" high, chrome plated body with walnut handles, browning control dial, off and on switch. Heat sensor light lights up when toaster is on and turns off when toaster shuts off. Toaster can be turned off and on manually. Note: It was advisable when toaster was not in use to always shut it off manually or unplug it for safety purposes. $55.00.

MONTGOMERY WARD

1930s, 7½" high, chrome body with Bakelite handles, no heat control. Marked on bottom: "248.115V 400W. pat. nos. 1.756. 784. 2.005, 364-2,029.575, model no. 84k.w. 2298B. Patents Pending, Montgomery Ward USA." Note: The knob on the left side is marked "TURN." When the knob is turned down toward you, it opens both doors at the same time; when turned back it closes both doors at once. $45.00 w/cord.

MONTGOMERY WARD

early 1930s, 7" high, chrome plated body with brown painted base and walnut handles. The coil heating elements are laced through porcelain hooks. Nameplate reads: "Montgomery Ward U.S.A. Volts 115 Watts 450 Cat. No. 5228 Pat. No. 2,029,575. 96,764. 2,003,367. Patents Applied For." $25.00.

MONTGOMERY WARD

1930s, 7⅛" high, chrome plated doors with painted black enamel body and base, black wooden handles, laced coil heating element. Marked on the bottom: "Montgomery Ward USA Volts 115 Watts 500 Cat. No. 5238 Pat No. Patents Applied For." $25.00.

MONTGOMERY WARD

(1 Slice) Oven Style, 1920s, 8" high, nickel plated body with ebonized knobs and wooden feet. Marked on the bottom: "Blue Line Trade Mark Montgomery Ward & Co. Volts 108/116 No. 63-896 Watts 550 Pat. Applied For." Toaster is operated by pushing the top lever down to the desired brownness number. Door is pushed back into the toaster manually. The upper lever moves up the numbered side to the switch button on top that is marked "Open" which releases and opens the door, and the toaster then shuts off automatically. $55.00.

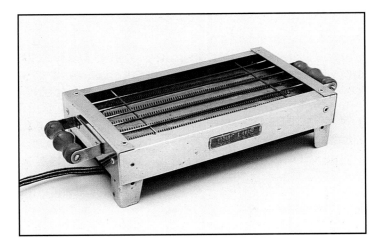

MONTGOMERY WARD

Toast Stove, 1920s, 2½" high by 11¾" long and 5¼" wide, nickel plated body and feet with blue wooden handles, laced coil heating element, no heat control. Front label reads: "Blue Line Montgomery Ward And Co. Volts 105-120 Watts 500." $30.00.

NCAT

late 1930s, 4-slice toaster, 7¼" high, manufacturer unmarked, chrome plated body with wooden door knobs and base carrying handles, 3-section mica heating element. Marked on the bottom: "NCAT 410A Volts 110-120 Watts 800." $35.00.

NELSON

late 1930s, 7¾" high, chrome plated doors with black painted sides and base, wafer handles. Marked on bottom: "Mfd. By The Nelson Machine & Mfg. Co. Cleveland Ohio, Cat. No. 94 Watts 500 Volt 110 Pat." $30.00.

Bottom:
NEW PERFECTION

1912, stove-top style toaster, 1⅝" high x 9" x 9", solid blue enamel ware base with black underside, black wooden handle, metal slide out toast rack. Each corner of the base is pierced. Marked on the side: "Pat'd. Nov. 25, 1912." Note: An advertisement from a 1917 New Perfection catalog reads: "Four Large Pieces Of Bread May Be Toasted At One Time, The Heat Is Distributed Over Entire Toasting Surface." $165.00.

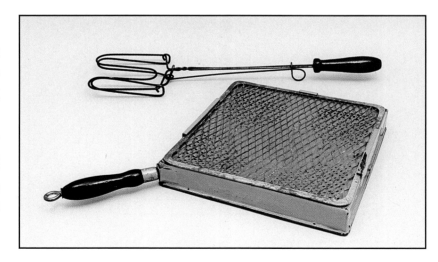

Top:
Toasting Fork, unmarked, early 1900s, 18½" long x 4¼" wide, wire with black wooden handle. Fork is operated by placing index finger in finger loop, then pulling it back to open the fork. Place bread in open fork, close, and hold over heat for toasting. After toast is done, procedure is repeated to remove toast from fork. $60.00

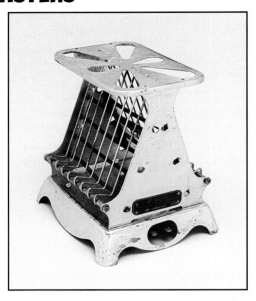

PACIFIC ELECTRIC HEATING CO.

El Toasto, early 1900s, 7" high, nickel plated body, horizontal laced wire coil heating element, no heat control, no moving parts. Bread rests on wire structure for toasting. Bread has to be turned manually. Side nameplate reads: "El Toasto Pacific. Electric Heating Co. Ontario, Cal. USA Chicago, USA Volts 110 No.11109190 Amps 5.6". $150.00.

OATLIN MFG. CO. INC.

Sandwich, 1920s, 5" high not including wooden base, base is 1⅝" high, nickel plated body with black wooden handle. Heat is controlled by off/on switch on front of wooden base. The red light shows when toaster is on. Marked on cover top "Oatlin Manufacturing Company Inc. Electrical Appliances Oatlin Illinois 110V 600W." Note: A wire encases the cord, which I believe helps to keep the cord away from the toaster. Because the toaster is mounted on a wooden base, I think this could be a store model. $135.00.

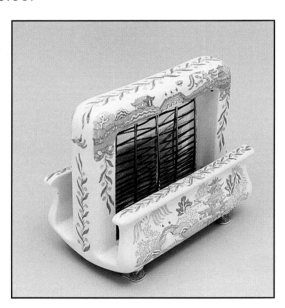

PAN ELECTRIC MFG. CO.

Toastrite, late 1920s – 1930s, 6¾" high, Blue Willow patterned porcelain body (in the red or pink coloring). Marked on bottom: "Toastrite 110 Volts 500 Watts The Pan Electric Manufacturing Co. Patented Cleveland. O." $3,500.00.

PAN ELECTRIC MFG. CO.

Toastrite, late 1920s – 1930s, 6¾" high, Blue Willow patterned porcelain body. Marked on bottom: "Toastrite 110 Volts 500 Watts The Pan Electric Mfg. Co. Patented Cleveland. O." $3,500.00.

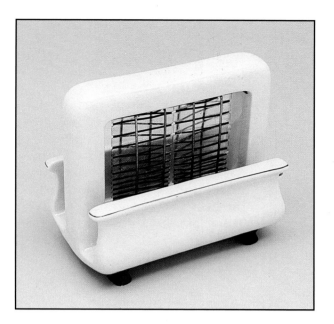

PAN ELECTRIC MFG. CO.

Toastrite, late 1920s – 1930s, 6¾" high, pearlized iridescent porcelain body. Marked on bottom: "Onyxide Toastrite 110 Volts Pan Electric Mfg. Corp. Patented Cleveland O." $1,600.00. Note: This toaster was also made in other iridescent colors such as blue, $1,600.00; yellow and green $1,600.00 each; orange $1,750.00.

PENN-AIR

late 1930s, 6¾" high, aluminum body with black Bakelite handles, wooden feet, no heat control. Marked on bottom: "Penna Aircraft Wks, Inc. Phila PA USA Penn-Air. UL 120V 275W Model 277A." $35.00.

THE PERFECTION ELECTRIC PRODUCTS CO.

Excelsior Twin Reversible, late 1920s, 7¾" high, highly polished nickel finish. Nameplate reads: "Excelsior Twin Reversible Toaster, The Perfection Electric Products Co. New Washington, Ohio. Manufactured Under Patents No. 1358, 932-1417,073. 4-7-A. 100-115 Other Patents Pending." Note: When the crank on the top of the toaster is turned, it rotates the two toaster baskets in opposite directions, pausing in center position for placing bread. The crank is then turned again to complete the cycle for the bread to be placed against the heating elements for toasting. The toast is then removed manually. $675.00.

PORCELIER MFG. CO.
serving set, three pieces, late 1930s, electric coffee pot, sugar, and creamer; coffee pot 13" high, sugar and creamer 5⅜" high, bodies are decorated porcelain. Coffee pot marked on bottom: "Porcelier Mfg. Co. Trade Mark Greensburg, PA USA Cat. No. 5007 115V 450W." $250.00 for three pieces.

PORCELIER MFG. CO.
serving set, three pieces, late 1930s, electric coffee urn, sugar, and creamer; coffee urn 13¾" high, sugar and creamer 5⅜" high, bodies are decorated porcelain. Coffee urn marked on bottom: "Porcelier Mfg. Co. Trade Mark Greensburg. PA USA Cat. No. 5009 115V 450W." $300.00 for three pieces.

PORCELIER MFG. CO.
late 1930s, 7¼" high, body is decorated porcelain. Marked on bottom: "Porcelier Mfg. Co. Trade Mark Greensburg, PA USA CAT No. 5002 115 V. 800W." The basketweave porcelain body is decorated with wildflowers decal designed by Emil Hasentab, a 1930s company designer. Note: On the left side is an off-on knob, when pushed down the toaster is turned on; on the front of the toaster is a controlled browning knob. When bread has reached desired browning, toaster is shut off automatically. $1,675.00.

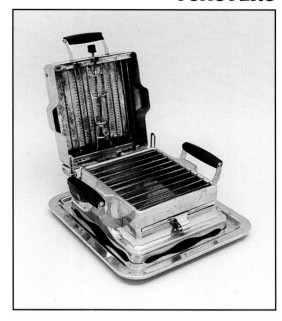

PRECISION MFG.
Rainbow, 1930s, 7⅜" high, chrome plated body with black wooden handles and feet, no heat control. Marked on the bottom: "Rainbow, Made By Precision Mfg. Dover, NJ USA 115V 500W." $40.00.

PROCTOR ELECTRIC CO.
Automatic in bottom photo, shown in open position. $95.00.

PROCTOR ELECTRIC CO.
1930s, 7¼" high, chrome plated body with black Bakelite handles and knobs, light and dark heat control. One door is marked on top edge: "Use This Door For One Slice." This door also has a cut-out arrow on top edge. The heat signal light on top of toaster, as well as the bell on bottom, lets you know when the toast is ready to be turned, by lowering the doors manually which turns the toast and resumes toasting. Marked on the bottom: "Proctor Thermostatic ToasterModel 1440C Alternating Current Only 500 Watts 110-120 Volts Proctor & Schwartz Electric Co. Philadelphia, PA USA Pat 1,481,021. 1,540,628 and Pending." $55.00.

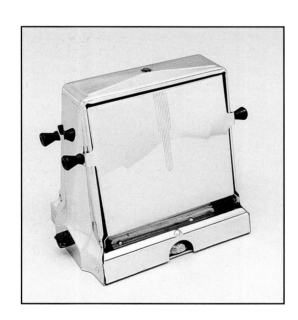

PROCTOR ELECTRIC CO.
Automatic, late 1920s, 4¼" high, nickel plated body and tray, with black Bakelite handles, dark and light heat control, removable crumb tray. Marked on the bottom: "Proctor Automatic Toaster No. 1405, 110 Volts - 600 Watts Use On Alternating Current Only. Patent No. 1540628 Other Patents Pending Made By Proctor & Schwartz Electric Co. Philadelphia, PA USA." $95.00.

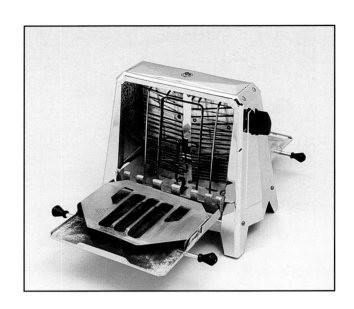

PROCTOR & SCHWARTZ ELECTRIC CO.
Glow-Cone Automatic, 1930s, 7⅛" high, chromium finish with black Bakelite handles and knobs. Marked on the bottom: "Proctor Glow-Cone Automatic Model No. 1420 Alternating Current Only. Pat. No. 1,540,628 and Pend. 500 Watts 110-120 Volts Proctor & Schwartz Electric Co., Philadelphia PA USA." $125.00.

PROCTOR & SCHWARTZ ELECTRIC CO.
Glow-Cone Automatic, shown in open position. On the right side is a dial that you can set light or dark. The Glow-Cone silently signals when toast is done. The current goes off and on automatically. The two slices of toast are kept warm without burning until served. The door shown was fitted with an inner section for toasting thin slices of bread. $125.00.

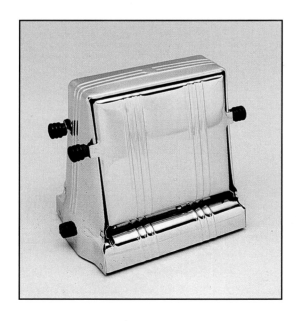

PROCTOR ELECTRIC CO.
Thermostatic, 1935, chrome body with black wooden door handles, Bakelite light and dark heat control knob, wafer feet. Top edge of one door is marked "Use This Side For One Slice." The heat is controlled by a thermostat and a bell rings when toast is done. The doors are operated by a spring controlled lever on the bottom of one side. Marked on the bottom: "Proctor Thermostatic Toaster Model 1444 Alternating Current Only. 500 Watts 110-120 Volts Proctor & Schwartz Electric Co. Philadelphia, PA. USA Pat 1540628 & Pending." $45.00.

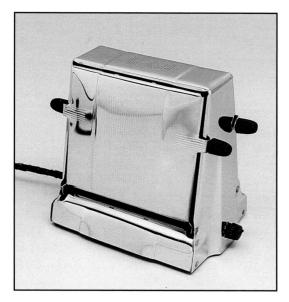

PROCTOR ELECTRIC CO.
1930s, 7" high, chrome plated body with black Bakelite handles and knob, wafer feet, light and dark heat control. One door is marked on the top edge: "Use This Side For One Slice." Marked on the bottom: "Proctor Thermostatic Toaster Model 1445 Alternating Current Only 450 Watts 110-120 Volts Proctor Electric Co. Philadelphia PA USA Pat 1,540,628. 2,079,382. 2,150,840. Also See Carton." $45.00.

PROCTOR ELECTRIC CO.
above toaster shown with one door open to show how the bread rests against the thermostat. The inside of the door also has three barrel-shaped rods, that when the door is shut, press the bread against the heating element. $45.00.

PROCTOR ELECTRIC CO.
1940s, 7" high, chrome body with Bakelite handles, knobs and base. Marked on the bottom: "Proctor Pop-up Automatic Toaster. Volts 110-120 No1471 1100 Watts Use On Alternating Current Only. Proctor Electric Co. Philadelphia Penna USA Pat. 1540628. 2179422. 2150640. Also See Carton." This toaster is advertised in a 1942 *Good Housekeeping* magazine as the "Proctor Dual-Automatic The Pop-up Toaster With The Crisper." This toaster is designed with a "Crisper" button for "Crispier, Crisp Or Soft." $40.00.

PROCTOR ELECTRIC CO.
late 1940s, 7⅛" high, chrome body with Chased ornament trim. Marked on bottom: "Proctor Automatic Pop-Up With Color Guard Toaster. Proctor Electric Co. Philadelphia 40 Penna, USA Model 1481 Patents 2,179,422. 2,301,070. 2,339-18. Also See Cartons. For Alternating Current Only. 110-120 Volts 1000 Watts." Note: The old Proctor ad from the 1940s, and how times have changed in how the housewife entertained. In the 1940s the toaster as well as the accessories was the center of attention at special occasions. $45.00.

Left: **PROCTOR ELECTRIC CO.**
Pop-Up, mid 1940s, 7¼" high, chrome body with brown Bakelite handles, knobs, and base, light and dark browning control. Top of toaster reads: "Use This Side For One Slice." Removable bottom crumb tray. Marked on the bottom: "Proctor Model 1466 Pop-Up Toaster Use On Alternating Current Only. (also a number of patents numbers listed.) Proctor Electric Company Philadelphia PA USA." $45.00.
Right: **PROCTOR ELECTRIC CO.**
Pop-Up, Same as at left except this toaster has black Bakelite handles, knobs, and base and is marked "PROCTOR" on the top. $45.00.

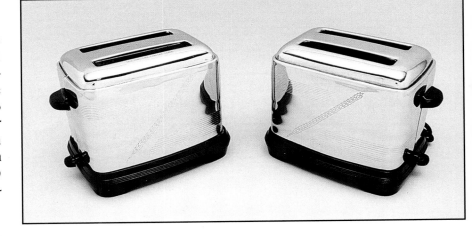

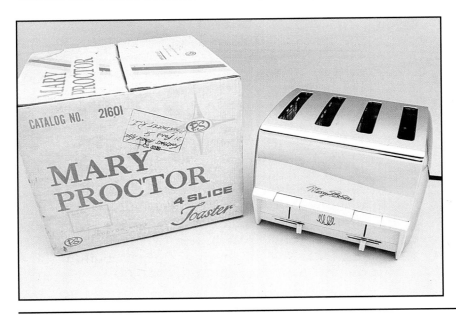

PROCTOR SILEX
Mary Proctor, late 1950s to 1960s, 4-slice automatic pop-up toaster with original box, 7⅜" high, chrome plated body with hard plastic base and knobs. Marked on the bottom: "Proctor Silex Corp. Phila, PA USA For Alternating Current Only. 120 Volts 1650 Watts Mary Proctor Automatic Pop-Up Toaster Model P21601 Guar Exp Dec 66." One individual slice can be toasted as well as two or four slices. Original box is marked on the bottom with several patent numbers and the design number 176,275, and also the dates in Canada 1955 – 1964. $95.00 with original box.

RENFREW
late 1920s, 8" high, chrome body with black Bakelite handles. Marked on bottom: "Renfrew Electric and Refrigerator Co. Ltd. 110V No. 406 5A N.E.P.C. App No. 103. Note: This toaster has flat cord prongs, $30.00. With original cord, $50.00.

REX-RAY
1930s, 6¾" high, chrome plated doors with painted brown enamel sides, top, and base, brown wooden handles, no heat control. Marked on the bottom: "Rex-Ray Appliances St. Louis USA Pat. Nos. 1,756,784. 2,005,364. 2,029,575. 115V 400W Cat. No. X-336 Pats. Pend." $30.00.

RIVERSIDE MFG. CO.
Aluminum toaster, 1930s, 6⅝" high, nickel plated body with painted black, rough textured base, black Bakelite door pulls, vertical laced open spring-coil heating element, no heat control. Model 1002, 110 Volts, 550 Watts, Mfg. by Riverside Mfg Co. Ypsilanti, Mi. $75.00.

ROCK ISLAND MFG.

Rimco, 1920s, 7¼" high, nickel plated body with black wooden handles, mica heating element. Nameplate reads: "Rimco 110 Volts 484 Watts #17A Made in the USA Rock Island Manufacturing Co. Rock Island, Ill. USA." Note: When the door is opened, two rods connected at the bottom side of each door pull the up and down toast rods away from the mica heating element so the bread can be toasted on the other side or removed. There is no controlled heat indicator, just the off-and-on switch at the base of the toaster. The attached weight at the base of the toaster helps stabilize the toaster when in use. $150.00

ROWENTA ELECTRIC

early 1900s, 3" high by 8¾" wide and 9⅜" long, nickel plated body with Bakelite feet, removable wire toast rack, holds four slices of bread. Marked on the side: "Rowenta E 5107 120 Volt 660 Watts." $30.00.

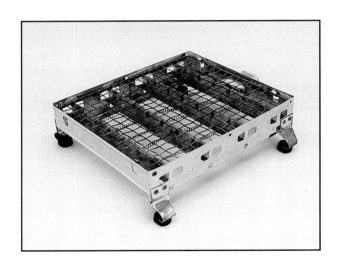

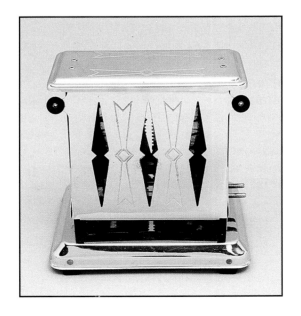

ROYAL BRAND

1920s, 7½" high, chrome plated body with fiber handles and feet, mica heating element, no heat control. Marked on the bottom: "Royal Brand Style No____ Volts 110-120 Watts 550. Royal Brand Products, New York." $45.00.

ROYAL ROCHESTER

1910, 6¾" high, nickel plated body with black wooden carrying handle, horizontal laced wire coil heating element over mica, no heat control. Nameplate reads: "Royal Rochester, Rochester Stamping Co. Royal Rochester. Rochester, New York. Volts 110 Patented No. 114 Amps 5." Note: How the bread rests against the wire structure for toasting. Bread has to be removed and turned manually. The "wheel" shaped top is designed to keep toast, or a coffee pot warm. (Coffee pot pictured is called Granite Ware blue and white "Columbian" ware. From author's collection.) Toaster $150.00.

Also pictured:

Toast Rack, 1920s, 7¾" high. Marked "Simpson H.M. & Co. 251." $55.00.

Left:

ROYAL ROCHESTER

1910 – 1915, 6⅝" high, polished nickel plated steel body. Nameplate reads: "Royal Rochester, Rochester Stamping Co. Rochester, New York. Volts 110 Patented No. 9-1, Amps 4.1 Lmp." This toaster has no heat control. The gravity operated bread clamps can be raised with a slice of bread. Racks are 4½" by 5¼", larger than the slices in a standard loaf. $125.00.

Right:

ROYAL ROCHESTER

1910 – 1915, 6⅝", high polished nickel plated steel body. Nameplate reads: "Royal Rochester, Pat. E6401 Lmp. Rochester Stamping Co. Made in Rochester NY USA. Note: The different tops on these two toasters, also the differences in the nameplate readings. $125.00.

ROYAL ROCHESTER

1929, 7⅝" high, chrome plated fancy doors with black body, base, and knobs, no heat control, mica heating element. Marked on the bottom: "E6414 Royal Rochester, Robeson Rochester Corp. Rochester, NY 110-120 Volts 450 Watts Pat. Pend. March 6, 1929." $55.00.

ROYAL ROCHESTER

1930s, 7⅜" high, chrome body with black Bakelite handles and feet, no heat control. Marked on bottom: "13260 Royal Rochester, Robeson Corp. Rochester, N.Y. 110-120 Volts 465 Watts." $55.00.

ROYAL ROCHESTER

1930s, 7⅛" high, chrome plated body with Bakelite handles, no heat control. Marked on the bottom: "Royal Rochester, Robeson Corp. Rochester, N.Y. 110-120 Volt 500 Watts. 13290." $50.00.

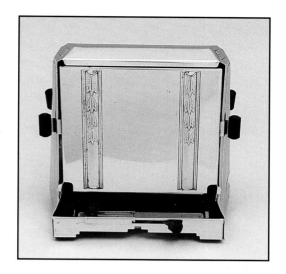

ROYAL ROCHESTER
late 1920s, 7⅜" high, chrome body with brown Bakelite handles and knobs. Marked on bottom: "Royal Rochester, Robeson Rochester Corp. Rochester N.Y. 110-120 Volts 500 Watts Cat. 13250." The controlled heat selector is numbered 1-6. When toast has browned, the timing bell rings and shuts off toaster. $45.00.

ROYAL ROCHESTER
mid 1930s, 7⅛" high, finish is "Non-Tarnishing Chromium". Marked on the bottom: "13340 Royal Rochester, Robeson Rochester Corp. Rochester, NY 110-120 Volts 500 Watts C33." In an old Royal Rochester catalog, dated October 15, 1936, this model is advertised as "The Lenox, finished entirely in gleaming non-tarnish chromium. Toast two slices of bread. Turn over feature. Four cool turning knobs. Non-Scratch fiber feet. Genuine mica-core element. Long detachable cord. Price (then) at $3.25." $40.00.

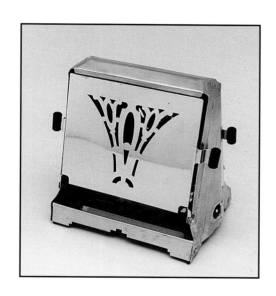

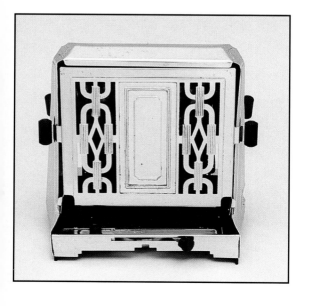

ROYAL ROCHESTER
mid 1930s, 7⅛" high, finished entirely in lustrous non-tarnishing chrome. Marked on the bottom: "A36 Royal Rochester, Robeson Corp. Rochester NY 110-120 Volts. Cat 13370. An old Royal Rochester catalog dated October 15, 1936, advertises this model as the "Signal Control Two Slice Toaster – The Aristocrat. Beautiful pierced and embossed design. New one-piece construction. It tells you when the toast is done, that's what you want to know. Simply set the degrees of brownness you prefer and when one side of toast is toasted (the signal bell tells you when), just lower the doors and bread turns automatically. Raise doors, set signal control lever and when the other side is perfectly toasted, the signal bell rings, that's your signal to take out two pieces of golden evenly browned toast. Price (then) $5.95." $50.00.

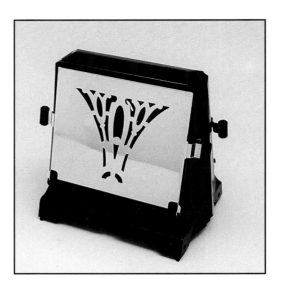

ROYAL ROCHESTER

mid 1930s, 7⅛" high, finished in lustrous chrome with black chrome sides and frame. Marked on the bottom: "13300 Royal Rochester, Robeson. Rochester Corp, Rochester, NY 110-120 Volts 500 Watts." An old Royal Rochester catalog dated October 15, 1936, advertises this model as "the DELUXE, finished in lustrous chrome and black chrome sides and frame. This combination is the newest and most acceptable trend in modern tableware, and this toaster is an exceptionally fast seller. Attractive pierced embossed design. Genuine mica-core element. Long detachable cord. Price (then) $3.50." $40.00.

ROYAL ROCHESTER

mid 1930s, 7⅛" high, finished in lustrous non-tarnishing chrome, with black chrome sides and frame, red Bakelite handles. Marked on the bottom: "D35 Royal Rochester, Robeson Rochester Corp. Rochester, NY 110-120 Volts 500 Watts Cat 13400." $40.00.

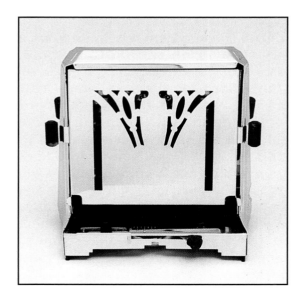

ROYAL ROCHESTER

mid 1930s, 7¼" high, non-tarnishing chromium finish with black Bakelite handles and wafer feet, heat control button marked from the 1-6 setting. When timing bell rings, it tells you toast is ready for turning or removing. Marked on the bottom: "Royal Rochester, Robeson Rochester Corp. Rochester, NY. 110-120 Volts 500 Watts Cat 13440." $50.00.

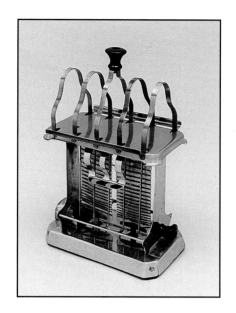

ROYAL ROCHESTER
pictured at left in the bottom photo on page 87, here shown with removable toast rack. This removable toast rack fits on toaster snugly. When removed, it makes a handy way to pass around the toast. Unmarked. Toast rack measures 4¾" high. Polished nickel plated steel with ebonized black handle. $200.00 with toast rack.

RUTENBER ELECTRIC CO.
Marion Giant Flip Flop, 1930s, 8" high, chrome plated body with fiber handles and molded feet, no heat control. Side nameplate reads: "Make Toast Your Breakfast Food With Marion Giant Flip Flop Model 66 Volts 110 Watts 550 Made By Rutenber Electric Co. Marion, Ind. Patented July 28, 1914 Made in USA." Note: The interior rack that holds the bread away from the heating element is hinged to the lower section of the outer door. When door is opened and pulled down, the lower section of the inner rack also swings out with the door, flipping the toast automatically. $55.00.

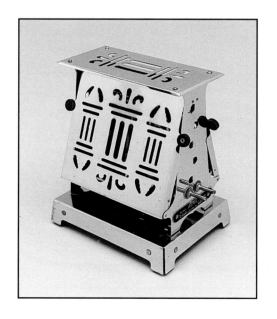

RUTENBER ELECTRIC CO.
Marion Super Flip Flop, 1930s, 8¼" high, chrome plated body with fiber handles and feet, no heat control. Side nameplate reads: "Marion Super Flip Flop Toaster. Trademark Reg. Model 67 Volts 110 Watts 550 Rutenber Electric Co. Marion, Ind. Patented July 28, 1914." $45.00.

RUTENBER ELECTRIC CO.

Model 60, early 1900s, 6¼" high, chrome body with white porcelain feet, no heat control. Marked on the side: "Rutenber Electric Company Logansport, Ind. USA Volts 110 Watts 500 MOD 60." Note: The mica is a solid piece panel screwed into an extra inner metal frame. The wire is laced in and out of holes through the solid one-piece mica panel. Bread is placed against the horizontal wires for toasting. The base of the toaster where bread sits is tilted down towards the center so bread will lean towards the heating element and not fall out. The cutouts on the top section help heat to escape and keep toast warm when toast is placed on top. $110.00.

SAMSON UNITED CORP.

Automatic, 1950s, 7⅝" high, chrome body with brown Bakelite handles, knobs, and base. Marked on the bottom: "Samson Automatic Toaster Model 5147N Made In USA By Samson United Corp. Rochester, N.Y. USA 1100 Watts 115 Volts. Operates On AC Only Patents Applied For." Bread is lowered into the toaster by turning the large center knob to the right. Toast can also be released by the Toast Release Button on the lower right side. $55.00.

SAMSON UNITED CORP.

Sandwich Grill, 1930s, 4" high by 16" long and 9¾" wide, chrome body with painted black decoration, and Bakelite handles, knob, and feet, no heat control. Marked on the bottom: "Samson No. 234 700W 115V Samson United Corp. Rochester, NY. Made in USA Patented Pats. Pending." (This piece is the companion piece to center photo on page 95.) $55.00.

SAMSON UNITED CORP.
Sandwich Toaster, late 1930s, 4⅛" high, chrome plated body with black Bakelite handles, and black wooden feet, no heat control. Marked on the bottom: "Samson No. 134 700W 115V Samson United Corp. Rochester, N.Y. Made in USA Patented-Pat's Pending." $45.00.

SAMSON UNITED CORP.
Tri-matic, late 1930s, 3-slice, 7⅞" high, chrome body with black enamel trim on top of toaster, Bakelite base and knobs. Marked on bottom: "No. 194 925W - 115 V Samson United Corp. Rochester, N.Y. Made in USA Patent Numbers 87,209. 2,059,440. Patents Pending 127." Note: This three-slice toaster has a light and dark button on back of toaster. When you push the upper release button on the right side, this brings the toast rack out for bread to be placed on. Toast rack is then pushed back into the toaster manually. The lower right timing arm is then pulled back to start toasting; when toasting time is completed, this arm springs forward and shuts toaster off automatically. You then push the upper release button for toast to come out on the racks. $225.00.

SAMSON UNITED CORP.
Tri-matic, late 1930s, 3-slice, 7⅞" high, chrome plated body with black enamel trim on top, Bakelite base and knobs. Marked on bottom: "No. 194 1100W-115V Samson United Corp. Rochester, N.Y. Made In USA. Patented-Pats Pending." Note: The difference in these two toasters is the button on back of this toaster which is marked ABCD instead of light and dark. When the toasting cycle is done and the toaster shuts off automatically, you continue to pull the timing arm towards you, and this brings the toast racks out. There is no upper button on this toaster to release the toast. $200.00.

SAMSON UNITED CORP.

1930s, 7⅝" high, chrome body with black wooden door pulls and feet, Bakelite heat control knob, mica heating element. Heat control is operated by pulling the lever to the left for "On". You then return the lever for degree of brownness. Toaster shuts off automatically. Marked on the bottom: "Samson No. 5052 115V 425W Samson United Corp. Rochester, N.Y. Made In USA Patent Numbers 2,008,799. 91180 S.U.C. No25 Use On AC Current Only. 79". $45.00.

SAMSON UNITED CORP.

1930s, 7¾" high, chrome plated body with black Bakelite handles and attached bottom tray. Marked on the bottom: "Samson No. 198 115V-550W Samson United Corp. Rochester, N.Y. Made In USA Patented and Pats. Pending." $55.00.

SAMSON UNITED CORP.

1930s, 7⅛" high, chrome plated body with walnut handles. Marked on the bottom: "Samson No. 5353, 115V 425W Samson United Corp. Rochester, N.Y. Made In USA Ser No. 29." $20.00.

SAMSON UNITED CORP.

1930s, 7⅛" high, chrome plated body with wooden handles and feet, no heat control. Marked on the bottom: "Samson No. 5353 115V 225W Samson United Corp. Rochester, N.Y. Made In USA Ser No. 29." $25.00.

SAMSON UNITED CORP.

1930s, 7¼", chrome body with painted black decorations on the doors, and black Bakelite handles and feet, no heat control. Marked on the bottom: "Samson No. 297 115V 425W Samson United Corp. Rochester, N.Y. Made In USA Patent numbers 91,180. 2,008,799. Patents Pending 77." $35.00.

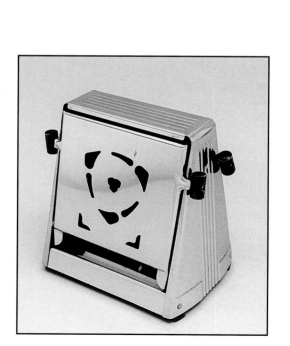

SENECA

1930s, 7½" high, chrome body with walnut handles, no heat control. Marked on the bottom: "Seneca No. 7051 115V 425 W Seneca Co. Brighton, NY Made in USA Patent Numbers 2,008,799. 91,180. Patents Pending 39." $40.00.

SIMPLEX ELECTRIC CO.

1909, 8⅞" high, highly polished nickel plated body, heavy metal black enamel base, black wooden carrying handle, ceramic core heating elements, never used. The double wall frame conceals the retractable wire toast warming rack on top of the toaster, which has to be pulled out manually. Toast also has to be turned manually. On the bottom side section of each removable door is a pin that fits into a slot on the double frame, which holds the doors onto the toaster. Marked on the bottom: "Simplex S.H. Co. Quality T-211 Volt 110 Amps 4.5 S482261." Manufactured by the Simplex Electric Co., Boston. Patent application filed October 1909, by James Ayer. $425.00.

SON-CHIEF ELECTRICS INC.

Forman 4 Family Inc. Buffet Server, 1930s. Coffee pot 10¾" high with genuine Pyrex glass liner and black Bakelite feet and handle. Marked: "4 Man Maid Chromium On Solid Brass Guaranteed Rustless, Volts 110-115 Watts 550, Patent No. 2,283,734 Forman 4 Family Inc. Brooklyn, NY Cat. 1000S." Covered jars, creamer, sugar, and fancy embossed serving tray with black Bakelite handles, are all unmarked. Serving tray is 27¼" long by 15½" wide. Tray has an attached 3-slice toast rack. Covered jars measure 1¼" deep by 4" square. Toaster 1930s, 7⅜" high, chrome body with black Bakelite handles, knobs and feet. Marked on the bottom: "Speed-O-Matic Watts 750 Volts 115 Son-Chief Electrics Inc. Winsted Conn. USA Series 612 AC Only." $325.00.

SON-CHIEF ELECTRICS INC.
Forman 4 Family Inc. Breakfast Server, 1930s. Coffee pot 10¾" high with genuine Pyrex liner and black Bakelite handles and feet. Marked: "Coffee 4 Man Maid 3 US Patents Pend Group AA No. 1000." Chromium on solid brass, guaranteed rustless. Volts 110-115 watts 550 4 Forman Bros, Inc. Brooklyn N.Y." Covered jars, sugar, creamer, and fancy embossed serving tray with black Bakelite handles and attached 3-slice toast rack are all not marked. Tray measures 20¼" long by 12¼" wide, each covered jar measures 1¼" deep by 4" square. Toaster, 1930s, 7⅜" high, chrome body with black Bakelite handles, knobs, and feet. Marked on the bottom: "Speed-O-Matic Watts 750 Volts 115 Son-Chief Electrics Inc. Winsted Conn. USA Series 612 AC Only." This breakfast server has the toast rack attached on the front edge of the tray, and the tray is not designed to hold the toaster. $295.00.

Left:
SON-CHIEF ELECTRICS INC.
Magic Maid, with original box, late 1930s, 7¼" high, chrome body with "New" vertical shaped handles. Marked on the bottom: "Son-Chief Series 680 Watts 550 Volts 115 Son-Chief Electrics Inc. Winsted, Conn. USA." This toaster has a smooth finish on the doors. On top of the original box is a sticker that reads: Silbey Lindsay, and Curr Co. $3.95. This company was one of the retailers for this toaster in Rochester, New York. This company no longer exists in Rochester. $70.00 with original box.

Right:
SON-CHIEF ELECTRICS INC.
Magic Maid, late 1930s, 7¼" high, same as the toaster on the left with the exception of the stippled finish on the doors. $20.00 without original box.

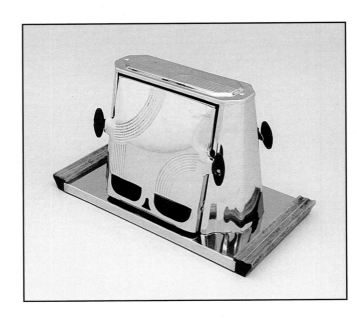

SON-CHIEF ELECTRICS INC.

Magi-Craft, 1940s, 7¼" high, chrome body with brown Bakelite handles and feet. Marked on bottom: "Magi-Craft Watts 750 Volts 115, AC Only Son-Chief Electrics Inc. Winsted, Conn. USA Model 677 Pop-up." $35.00.

SON-CHIEF ELECTRICS INC.

Son-Chief, 1930s, 7⅛" high, chrome plated body with wooden carrying and door handles, no heat control. Marked on the bottom: "Son-Chief Series 680 Watts 550 Volts 115 Son-Chief Electrics Inc. Winsted, Conn. USA." $35.00.

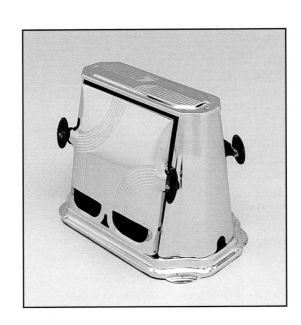

SON-CHIEF ELECTRICS INC.

Son-Chief, 1930s, 7½" high, chrome body with black Bakelite carrying handles, knobs, and feet, no heat control. Bread is lowered and raised by turning knob on side. Marked on the bottom: "Son-Chief Toast Oven Watts 660 Volts 115 Son-Chief Electrics Inc. Winsted, Conn. USA Series 611." $45.00.

SON-CHIEF ELECTRICS INC.

Son-Chief, 1930s, 7¼" high, chrome body with black wooden handles, flip-flop style, no heat control. Marked on the bottom: "Son-Chief Series 680 Watts 550 Volts 115 Son-Chief Electrics Inc. Winsted, Conn. USA SA UL." $30.00.

SON-CHIEF ELECTRICS INC.

Son-Chief, late 1930s, 7¼" high, chrome plated body with black Bakelite knobs, handles, and feet, light and dark heat control, pops toast up when done and shuts toaster off automatically. Marked on bottom: "Son-Chief Watts 750 Volts 115 Son-Chief Electrics Inc. Winsted, Conn. USA Series 622 AC Only." $45.00.

SON-CHIEF ELECTRICS INC.

Son-Chief Extra Fast, late 1920s, 7⅛" high, chrome body with molded feet, fiber door pulls, vertical laced wire coil heating element, no heat control. Stamped on the bottom: "Son-Chief Extra Fast Toaster Winsted, Conn." The bottom of this toaster is stamped with a faint ink type stamp. $40.00.

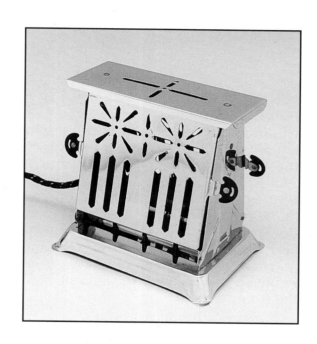

SON-CHIEF ELECTRICS INC.

Son-Chief Speed Master, 1930s, 7¼" high, chrome plated body with walnut carrying handles and door handles, no heat control. Marked on the bottom: "Speed Master Series 680 Watts 550 Volts 115 Son-Chief Electrics Inc. Winsted, Conn. USA." Note: I believe the purpose of the added base tray was to stabilize the toaster while in use. $35.00.

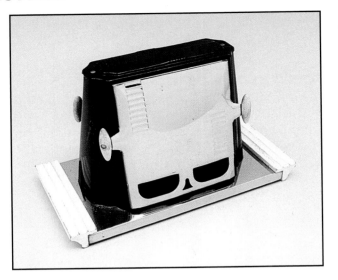

SON-CHIEF ELECTRICS INC.
Son-Chief Speed Master, late 1930s, 7¼"
high, chrome plated body with white
wooden carrying and door handles.
Marked on the bottom: "Speed Master
Series 680 Watts 550 Volts 115 Son-
Chief Electrics Inc. Winsted, Conn.
USA." $35.00.

SON-CHIEF ELECTRICS INC.
Son-Chief Speed-O-Matic, 1930s, 7⅜" high,
chrome body with black Bakelite handles and
knobs, dark and light heat control. Marked on
the bottom: "Speed-O-Matic Watts 750 Volts
115 Son-Chief Electrics Inc. Winsted, Conn.
USA Series 612 AC Only." Note: When the
knob on the front of the toaster is pushed
down, this lowers the bread into the toaster
and turns it on. When desired brownness is
reached, toaster shuts off. Toast is raised and
removed manually by pushing up the knob on
the front. $55.00.

SON-CHIEF ELECTRICS INC.
Son-Chief Speed-O-Matic, with origi-
nal box, 1930s, 7⅜" high, chrome
finish with black Bakelite handles,
knobs, and feet. Fully automatic.
Marked on the bottom: "Speed-O-
Matic Watts 750 Volts 115 Son-Chief
Electrics Inc. Winsted, Conn. USA
Series 612 AC Only." $110.00 with
original box.

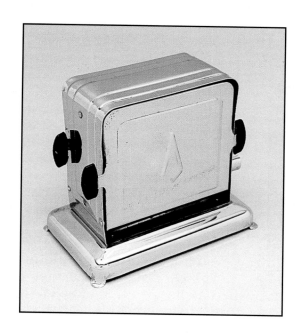

STANDARD APPLIANCE MFG. CO. LTD.

T-52, 1930s, 7¼" high, chrome body with molded chrome feet, black Bakelite handles, mica elements w/no heat control. Marked on bottom: "Standard Appliance Mfg. Co. Ltd. Toronto Canada SB 115V Cat. No. T-52 440 Watts." $35.00.

STEELCRAFT

late 1920s, 8" high, black wire constructed body, mica heating element, no heat control, red painted wood handles. Marked on the bottom of the power junction box: "Steelcraft K.C. Mo. 115V 550W Pat. Pending." $95.00.

SUNBEAM CORPORATION

Hostess Tray Set, 1930s – early 1940s, toaster is 7⅝" high, chrome body with black Bakelite handles and base, has red signal light. Toaster marked on the bottom: "Sunbeam Model T-9 Made in the United States of America Sunbeam Corporation Chicago USA Toronto, Canada, Pat 1,862,733. 2,031,656. 2,196,393. 2,197,221. 2,254,687. 2,271,485. Other Patents Pending, Canada Patented 1942-44- CSA Approval No. 8402 Volts 110-120 Watts 1100." Note: This toaster has a "light and dark" heat control; later models were marked "lighter and darker." The toaster is set and the red signal light tells you when the toast is done, but if you don't want the toast to pop-up, it will remain warm in the toaster. The circular chrome-plated tray with satin finish and the three compartment appetizer dish are not marked. $275.00.

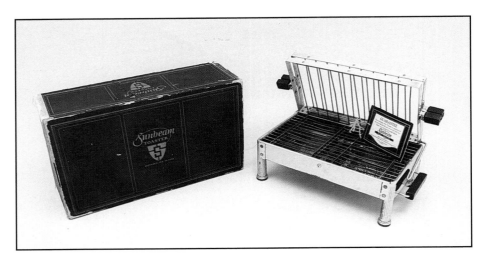

SUNBEAM CORPORATION

Flat Toaster, with original box, and cord, early 1920s, 4" by 5" by 9", chrome body. Marked on the attached back plug cover: "Sunbeam Model B Patented Jan. 30, 1923 Volt 110 Watts 600." The enclosed guarantee card states: "Bread placed directly over the heat makes a vast difference. The Sunbeam toaster toasts bread flat, the scientific way. The heat rises directly against the bread which is quickly changed into crispy hot toast. Toast can be flipped manually by swinging the toast baskets up and over by the handles. An arm attached on each end of the base allows the baskets to swing up and over. The end carrying handles on the base fold under the toaster." The box reads: "Sunbeam Toaster Patented Jan. 30, 1923. Made and Guaranteed By Chicago Flexible Shaft Company 37 Years Making Quality Products. Catalog No. B340." $125.00 with original box, cord, and guarantee card.

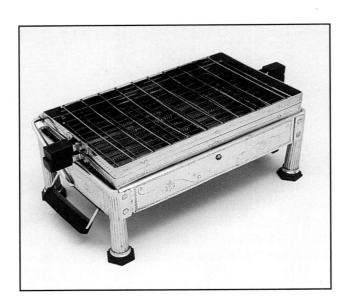

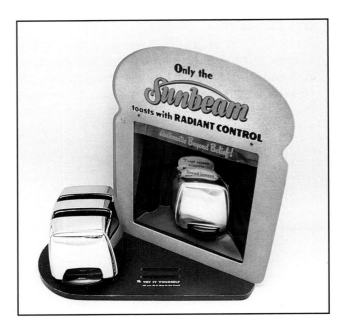

SUNBEAM CORPORATION

Flat Toaster, early 1920s, 4" by 5" by 9", "Imitation Engraved" chrome body, black Bakelite handles and feet. Marked on attached back plug cover: "Sunbeam Model B Patent 1,465,007 Volts 110 Watts 600." $55.00.

1949 Sunbeam Electric display featuring the Radiant Control Toaster, and how it works. Display background measures 22½" high and 17¾" wide. Bottom board is 22" long. Bread lowers automatically. No levers to push. "Toast raises silently, no popping or banging." Sunbeam Toaster is 7⅝" high. Marked on the bottom: "Sunbeam Model T-20B Made in the United States Of America. Sunbeam Corp. Chicago USA, Toronto, Canada." $425.00 complete with toaster.

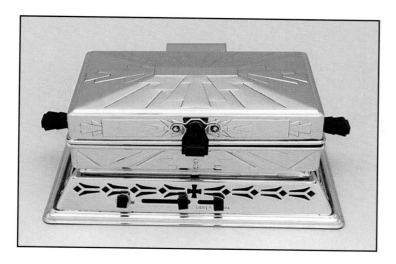

SUNBEAM CORPORATION

Toastwich, early 1930s, 4⅝" high by 10¾" long and 7¼" wide, chromium plated throughout, richly polished with black Bakelite handles. Marked on the back "Sunbeam Toastwich No. B5 Chicago Flexible Shaft Company. Chicago USA Patents Applied For. Volts 110-120 Watts 660 Chicago Oct. 20, 1930." The Sunbeam catalog No. 41-C pictures and advertises this Sunbeam Toastwich as "Completely automatic. Makes toast and toasts sandwiches too. Put the bread in, close the toaster, when done it shuts off the current, opens up itself, and raises up the front edge of the toast, so it can be picked off comfortably. It also keeps the toast warm until needed. The heating element structure raises up so that the reflector plate can be wiped off easily. Beautifully and artistically done. Comes complete with full length cord and plug." $165.00.

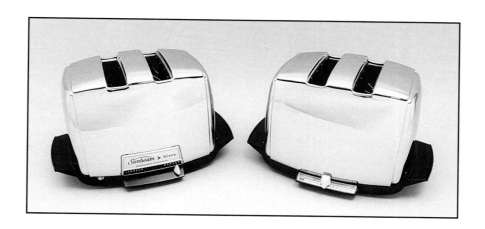

Left:
SUNBEAM CORPORATION

Vista Radiant Control, 1950s, 7½" high, chrome plated body with black carrying handles and base, light and dark heat control. Marked on top: "One Slice." Also marked on the bottom: "Sunbeam Model VT-40-1 Made in United States of America, Sunbeam Corporation Chicago, USA. (several patent numbers are listed.) Patent Pending, Volts 120 Watts 1375 For AC Only." This Sunbeam Vista Radiant Control toaster automatically lowers the bread for toasting and raises it back up when the toast is done. No levers to push. $30.00

Right:
SUNBEAM CORPORATION

1950s, 7½" high, chrome plated body with black carrying handles and base, "Shade Control" light and dark. Marked on top: "One Slice." Marked on the bottom: "Sunbeam Service At M, Made in United States of America Sunbeam Corporation Chicago USA. (several patent numbers are listed.) Patents Pending. Volts 120 Watts 1375 For AC Only." $30.00.

SUNBEAM CORPORATION
1930s, 7³⁄₈" high, chrome body with black Bakelite handles and base, high and low heat indicator on lower right side. The heat indicator light on front shuts off when toast is done. Marked on bottom: "Sunbeam, Chicago Flexible Shaft Co. Chicago, USA Model T-1A Volts 110-120 Watts 875." $70.00.

SUNBEAM CORPORATION
2-Piece Hospitality Set, 1930s, toaster is 7¼" high, chrome plated body with black Bakelite handles and base. Marked on bottom: "Sunbeam, Chicago Flexible Shaft Co. Chicago USA Model T-1-E DES. Pat 98247 Volts 110-120 Watts 875." Glass tray measures 1" deep x 11" wide x 16" long. Note: The one-piece glass tray has molded sections designed especially for the shape of the toaster, plus five other sections. $225.00 complete with glass tray.

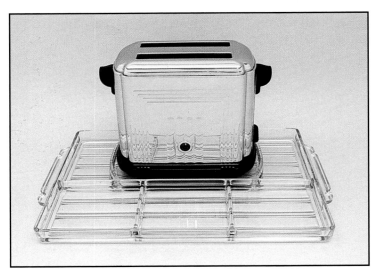

SUPERIOR ELECT. PROD. CORP.
Superlectric, late 1920s, 6¾" high, chrome body with black wafer door pulls, no heat control, mica heating element. Marked on the bottom: "Superlectric 110-120 Volts A.C. Or D.C. Mfd. By Superior Electric Prod. Corp. St. Louis Mo. Toaster No. 88 Series. 500 Watts." $45.00.

SUPERIOR ELECT. PROD. CORP.

Superlectric, late 1920s, 7⅜" high, chrome body with black Bakelite teardrop handles. Marked on bottom "110-120 Volts Superlectric AC or DC Superior Elec. Prod. Corp. St. Louis Mo. #333 Series, 5.4 Amps." Note: There are no heat controls. When the toast is done, it has to be released manually by pushing the lever on the left hand side down. This unusual eight-sided toaster is hard to find. $125.00.

SUPERIOR ELECT. PROD. CORP.

Superlectric, 1930s, 7½" high, chrome plated body with black Bakelite handles, wafer feet, mica heating element, no heat control. Marked on the bottom: "Super Lectric 110-120 Volts AC or DC Mfd. By Superior Elec. Prod. Corp. St. Louis Mo. Toaster No. 11 Series 4 Amps." $35.00.

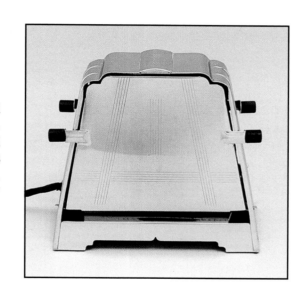

SUPERIOR ELECT. PROD. CORP.

Superlectric, 1930s, 7⅝" high, black painted body with chrome doors and top decoration, black Bakelite handles and wafer feet, mica heating element, no heat control. Marked on the bottom: "Superlectric 110-120 Volts AC Or DC Mfd. By Superior Elec Prod. Corp. St. Louis Mo., Toaster No. 11 Series 4 Amps." $35.00.

SUPERIOR ELECT. PROD. CORP.

Superlectric, 1930s, 7¾" high, chrome body with brown wooden door handles and feet, mica heating element, no heat control. Marked on the bottom: "Superlectric Volts 110-120 AC or DC Mfd. By Superior Elec. Prod. Corp. St. Louis Mo. No. 65 Series 3.5 Amp." $35.00.

SUPERIOR ELECT. PROD. CORP.

Superlectric, late 1930s, 7⅝" high, chrome plated body with black Bakelite handles and base. Marked on bottom: "Superlectric 110-120 Volts AC or DC Mfg. By Superior Elec. Prod. Corp. St. Louis Mo. No. 22 Series 16 Amp." $75.00.

SUPERIOR ELECT. PROD. CORP.

Superlectric Toaster Oven Combination, late 1940s, 10⅜" high, chrome plated body with Bakelite handles and feet. Nameplate reads: "Toaster-Oven 110-120V Watts 700 AC Only. Model No. 550 Superior Elec Prod. Corp. Cape Girardeau, Mo." Note: The red knob on the side snaps up to operate toaster, and down to operate oven. Lower oven is operated by preheating the oven empty and letting it go through one heating cycle before use. $175.00.

SUPERSTAR

1930s, 7⅛" high, nickel plated body with black wafer door pulls. Marked on the bottom: "Superstar Made in USA New York, New York. 475W 110V." $45.00.

SUPERSTAR

late 1930s, 7½" high, chrome plated body with walnut handles. Marked on the bottom: "Superstar Made in USA 500W 115V AC/DC." Note: This toaster is shown in a Stern-Brown catalog stamped June 26, 1939. This company was located at 42-44 Orchard Street, Long Island City, New York, NY USA and states this toaster is a No. 45 uniquely designed. Toast automatically reverses itself when lowering doors. Genuine India mica element covered with Nichrome ribbon. Special note: This toaster matches the Superstar Thermo Mastergrill below. $35.00.

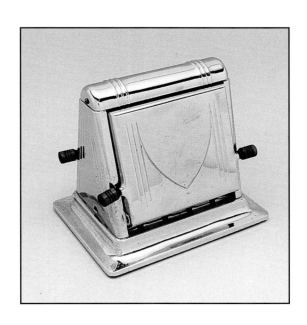

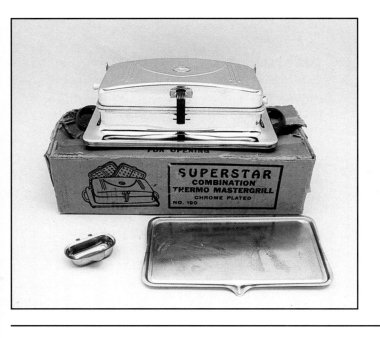

SUPERSTAR

Thermo Mastergrill, w/original box, late 1930s, size overall 14½" long, 7⁹⁄₁₆" wide, 4⅛" high. Marked on bottom: "Superstar Made in USA Long Island City NY Mastergrill Pat. Pend. 115V 525W AC/DC." Shown in the Stern-Brown catalog stamped June 26, 1939. Advertisement states "uniquely designed with brown ebonized trimmings, luxuriously chrome plated, will not tarnish. Genuine Nichrome heating unit. Sandwich Toaster Thermo Mastergrill will toast two or three slices of bread, double and triple deck sandwiches, also serves as a double grill stove and waffle grid. Removable drip cup takes care of excessive grease, etc..." $100.00 with original box.

SUPERSTAR

Toastrite, 1939, 7⅛" high, chromium plated body with walnut base and trim, adjustable control knob for browning, toast pops up when done and current shuts off, removable side crumb tray. Marked on the bottom: "Superstar Toastrite Made in L.I.C. N.Y. U.S.A. 115V 575W." $55.00.

SUPERSTAR

Toastrite Pop-Up, 1940s, 7¼" high, chrome plated body with brown Bakelite handles, knobs and base, light and dark heat control, slide out crumb tray. Marked on the bottom: "8-48 Superstar Toastrite Made In L.I.C. N.Y. 115V 575W AC or DC." $40.00.

TOASTMASTER

3-Slice, 1950s, 7⅛" high, chrome plated body with brown handles and feet. Marked on the bottom: "Toastmaster US Pat. Off. Super Deluxe Automatic Pop-Up Toaster 110-120 Volts 12 Amps Mod. 104 Operates on 50-60 Cycles Manufactured By Toastmaster Division McGraw-Edison Company Elgin, Illinois, USA (also lists a number of US patents), Patented in Canada 1942, 1944, 1953, 1955, Canada DES, RD 1953." $30.00.

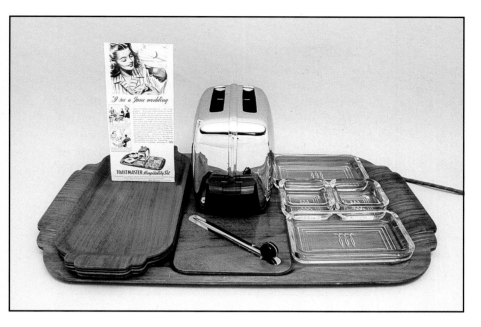

TOASTMASTER

7-Piece Hospitality Set, late 1930s. Toastmaster measures 7³⁄₈" high. Marked on bottom: "Toastmaster Reg US Pat. Off. Automatic Pop-Up Toaster Manufactured By Toastmaster Products. Div. McGraw Electric Company, Elgin ILL., USA. US Pat. No.'s 1,923,590-2, 001,362-2, 031, 656-2, 036, 178-2, 039, 956-2, 147, 388-2, 167, 121-2, 180, 232-2, 180, 233-2, 234,759-2, 266,024. 110-120 Volts 10.5 Amps. No. A 0630730. MOD 1B14 Operates on AC or DC. UL." Note: The old ad from a 1941 *Good Housekeeping* shows this deluxe hospitality set that sold for $23.95, included the walnut tray, four personal lap trays that are marked on the bottom: "Toastmaster Hospitality Tray, McGraw Electric Company, Toastmaster Products Division, Minneapolis, Minn. USA Patent Pending," stunning heavy-crystal appetizer dishes, clever toast trimmer, and the Toastmaster toaster. Also note that this set, along with the standard set that sold for $19.95, was advertised as a gift for June weddings. $325.00. Note: To find these sets complete is a rarity.

TOASTMASTER

Hospitality Set, late 1930s, toaster is 6⁷⁄₈" high. Nameplate on the bottom reads: "Manufactured By McGraw Electric Company Toastmaster Products Division. Mpls, Minn. USA US Pat. 1,698,146. 1,394,450. 1,387,670. 2,001,362. 1,866,808. 2,036,178, RE 18,923. Others Pending 110V - 10A - NO943426 MOD 1B6." Set includes four walnut lap trays that measure 15⁷⁄₈" long x 7½" wide. Main walnut hospitality tray measures 26" long x 15⁵⁄₈" wide. The 2-sectioned Duncan glass dishes

have the same pattern as the toaster and measure 7¾" x 6¾". The toast trimmer-slicer is designed to fit around the bottom section of the toaster. This Toastmaster Hospitality set was advertised in 1937 for the Christmas trade. It could also be purchased with a fold-up stand. $325.00.

TOASTMASTER

One-Slice, late 1930s, 7⅛" high, chrome plated body with brown Bakelite handles, knob, and base. Marked on the bottom: "Toastmaster Reg. US Pat. Office Mfg. By McGraw Electric Company Toastmaster Products Div. Elgin, Ill. USA. (several patent numbers listed), 110V 650 W NOK 1020472, MOD 1A5." $30.00.

TOASTMASTER

1930s, 6⅛" high, chrome body with black Bakelite handles and feet. Marked on the bottom: "Manufactured By McGraw Electric Company. Toastmaster Products Div. Minneapolis, Minn. USA 110V-8-No. MOD-187." $55.00.

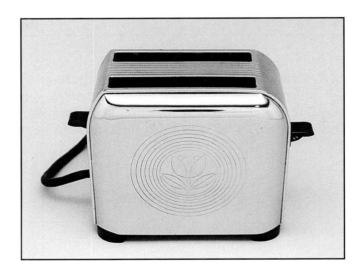

TOASTMASTER

late 1940s – early 1950s, 6" high, chrome plated body with brown Bakelite handles and feet. Marked on the bottom: "Toastmaster Automatic Pop-Up Toaster Model 1A6 Reg. US Pat. Off. McGraw Electric Co. Elgin Ill. USA US Pat. No.'s (patent numbers listed). Patented In Canada 1942 & 1944, 1953 & RD1953, 110-120 Volts AC Only 4.8 Amps Ser 0112342." $30.00.

TOASTWELL

1940s, 7⅛" high, chrome plated body with Bakelite handles and feet. Handle on the right side is marked "Toastwell." Also on one side is a dark and light lever. Marked on the bottom: "Cat. No. 885 The Toastwell Company. St. Louis Mo. 110-120V 920W A.C. Only. (several patent numbers listed) Other pats. pending. App. No. 3359." Note: The unique shape of this toaster, which resembles a loaf of bread. $65.00.

TOASTWELL

Pop-Up Toastwell, early 1940s, 6⅞" high, chrome plated body with Bakelite handles and base. Marked on bottom: "Pop-Up Toastwell N222-46 825W 110V Pats. 2,120,289-1, 884, 825-1, 914,649-DES115, 630-2, 049, 717-2, 112, 42-2. Other Pats. Pending. C.S.A. App. No. 3359 The Toastwell Company." Note: The unique shape of this toaster is like a loaf of bread. $65.00.

TOASTWELL

late 1940s, 6¾" high, chrome body with black Bakelite handles and feet. Marked on the bottom: "The Toastwell Company St. Louis Mo. 110-120V 920W Pat. Nos. 2,540,828; 2,049,717; 2,222,253; 6,372,274; 7,242,317; 2,336,696. Other Pats. Trademark Reg. USA App. No. 3359 UL." Metal lever attached to handle on right side controls browning cycle. Pops up automatically. The shape of this toaster reminds me of a loaf of bread. $65.00.

UTILITY ELECTRIC CO.
Automatic Toastwell, 1930s, 7¼" high, chrome body with green wooden knobs. Nameplate reads: "The Automatic Toastwell Patents Pending A.B.C.D.E.F.G. High-Low." Marked on the bottom: "Utility Electric Company St. Louis Mo. 600W Patents Applied." Note: The automatic browning lever on the lower right side is set to a desired browning time. Then the high and low lever is set for high or low heat. When bread is browned to the desired time required, the high and low lever snaps back, rings the bell, and shuts the toaster off. Each toast basket is raised separately, the toast is then raised and removed manually. $165.00.

UTILITY ELECTRIC CO.
Toastwell, non-automatic, mid 1930s, 7" high, chrome plated body with black Bakelite handles and feet, no heat control. Marked on the bottom: "Cat. No. 740 Non Automatic 660W 110V Utility Electric Company St. Louis Mo. Pats 1884825-1914649 Other Pats. Pending." $95.00.

UTILITY ELECTRIC CO.
Toastwell Automatic, 1939, 7¼" high, chrome body with Bakelite handles, knobs, and feet, light and dark control knob. Marked on the bottom: "H.E.P. C3359 Cat. No. 791 Automatic 660W 110V Utility Electric Co. St. Louis, Mo. 2,112,422 Pat. 1,884,825 1,914,649 Other Pats. Pend. 2,049,717." Note: Toast can also be released manually by turning the handle on the left sideways. Bell rings when toast is done. $75.00.

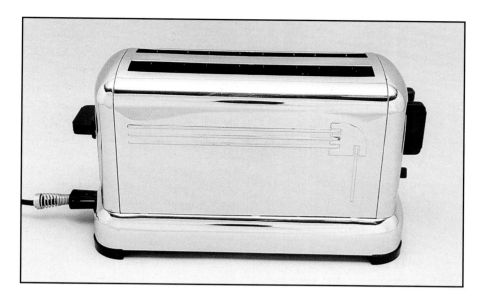

UTILITY ELECTRIC CO.

Toastwell Automatic, 4 slice, 1930s, 7¼" high, chrome body with black Bakelite handles and knobs. This fully automatic toaster has some really unique built-in features such as a selective automatic lift, raising toast to 5 intermediate levels for different purposes. These would include just grasping the toast and for those who prefer the toast left in the toaster to keep it piping hot until served and so on. Marked on the bottom: "Lift High & Low H.E.P.C. App. No. 3359 Cat. No. 795 Automatic Utility Electric Co. St. Louis, Mo. 2,112,422 Pats. 1884825-1914649 Other Pats. Pend. 2,049,717." $125.00.

VULCAN

early 1900s, stove-top non-electric, 5" high, tin with perforated metal center. Top marked: "Vulcan Toaster. No. 192 Pat'd. Apld. For." Note: I find these stove-top non-electric toasters interesting in the fact that most of today's generation and the generations to follow will not imagine what they were used for without an explanation. $45.00.

TOASTERS

WATERS-GENTER CO.

Toastmaster, 3-slice automatic, 1920s, 9⅞" high, heavy metal body with black knobs on left side. One knob operates the pop-up arm and the other regulates the degree of brownness. Nameplate on the side reads "3-Slice Automatic Toaster Strite US Pat. 1,387,670 Aug. 16, 21 1,394, 450 Oct. 18, 21 The Toastmaster, Model 1-C-1 Volts 110-220 Watts 2,200 No. 47000 Mfd. By Waters Genter Co. Minneapolis USA." This 3-slice commercial pop-up toaster was used mostly in restaurants and diners. These are referred to as "diner toasters" by collectors. $85.00.

WATERS-GENTER CO.

Toastmaster, late 1920s, 1-slice, 7½" high, chrome plated body with Bakelite knobs. Side nameplate reads: "Automatic Electric Toaster US Pat. Nos. 1,387,670; 1,394,450; 1,676,257. Others Pend. The Toastmaster Model 1-A-1 V110 W600 NO386821 Waters-Genter Co. Minneapolis, USA." Note: The small metal knob, below the larger Bakelite one on the right, is pulled out and set back into a grooved slot to the desired browning letter from A to G. Top lever is then pushed down, to the metal knob. This sets the browning time. When the lever on the left is pushed down, it lowers the bread and turns the toaster on. This Toastmaster Model1-A-1 is the first pop-up toaster made for home use by Waters-Genter Company from 1926 – 1929. $65.00.

WATERS-GENTER CO.

Toastmaster, 1930s, 7" high, chrome body with black Bakelite handles and feet. Nameplate reads: "Manufactured By McGraw Electric Company Waters-Genter Div. Mpls Minn. USA US Pat. 1,698,146; 1,387,670; 1,394,450; 1,676,257; 1,866,808; RE 18923. Others Pending V100 W600 No. K.837546 MOD 1A4." This toaster is fully automatic. $60.00.

WATERS-GENTER CO.

Toastmaster, 1930s, 7" high, chrome body with black Bakelite knobs. Nameplate reads: "Mfd. By Waters-Genter Co. Mpls. Minn. USA US Pat. 1,698,146; 1,387,670; 1,394,450; 1,676,257; 1,866,808. Others Pending V110 W600 NO.K734859 MOD-1A3." Old Toastmaster ads from the 1930s state that: "The One Slice Toastmaster Is Faster Than Most Two Slice Toasters, and It's Fully Automatic." $60.00.

WATERS-GENTER CO.

Toastmaster, 1930s, 7" high, chrome body. Nameplate reads: "Mfd. By Waters-Genter Co. Mpls, Minn. USA V110 A.9.8-118 No.180933 MOD 1B3." Low and light settings are also marked on the bottom. This two-slice toaster is fully automatic. $75.00.

WESTINGHOUSE

1914 – 1925, 7½" high, polished nickel body with fiber handles and feet. Marked on the bottom: "Westinghouse Turnover Toaster Cat. TT-3 110V 550W Pat 7-28-14-8-25-14 Westinghouse Elec. and Manufacturing Company Mansfield Works, Mansfield Ohio, USA." Note: The difference in design of this "TT-3" from the other "TT-3s", the fancy cutout fiber handles, and the design of the doors and the top. $40.00.

TOASTERS

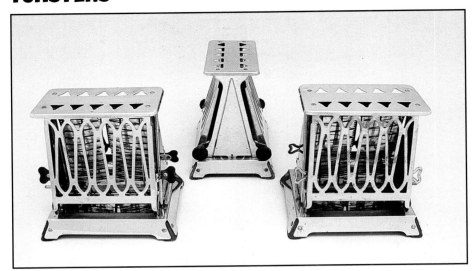

Left:
WESTINGHOUSE
1914 – 1920s, 7½" high, highly polished nickel. Marked on the bottom: "Westinghouse Turnover Toaster Cat. No. TT-3. 110V 550W Pat 7-28-14-8-25-14 Westinghouse Electric and Manufacturing Company Mansfield Works, Mansfield Ohio, USA." Note: The three views show the different style handles on each toaster. The first has the fiber handles and feet. All three toasters are Westinghouse Turnover Toasters. $40.00.

Center:
WESTINGHOUSE
1914 – 1920s, 7½" high. Same as the toaster on the left and marked the same on the bottom with the exceptions: "S#414414. Volts 110-120." This toaster has the ebonized knobs. $40.00.

Right:
WESTINGHOUSE
1914 – 1920s, 7½" high. Same as the toaster on the left, except that it has the cool metal handles. Note: The flat open design surface on top of these toasters can be used for warming toast, coffee, or plates. Each door is operated manually and separately by lowering or raising the doors with the handles or knobs on each side of the door. $40.00.

WESTINGHOUSE
Aristocrat Turnover Toaster, 1930s, unmarked, 7⅜" high, nickel plated body, fiber door pulls and feet, mica heating element, no heat control. $50.00.

WESTINGHOUSE
Turnover, 1925 – 1928, 7½" high, chrome plated body with fiber handles and feet. Marked on the bottom: "Westinghouse Turnover Toaster Cat. No. TTC-74 115V 550W Pat. 7-28-14, 8-25-14 Westinghouse Elec. and Manufacturing Company Mansfield Works, Mansfield Ohio, USA." $45.00.

WESTINGHOUSE

1930s, 7" high, chrome plated body with black wooden handles and black Bakelite feet, no heat control, mica element. Marked on the bottom: "Cat TT-72 115V 450W Westinghouse Mansfield Ohio Made In USA." $45.00.

WESTINGHOUSE

late 1930s, 7¼" high, chrome plated body with black wooden handles and fiber feet, no heat control. Marked on the bottom: "Cat. No. TL-14 450W 115V Westinghouse, Mansfield, Ohio Made in USA Patent 2093518. Also See Carton." $30.00.

WESTINGHOUSE

1940s, 7¼" high, chrome plated body with black Bakelite handles, knobs, and base, automatic. Marked on the bottom: "N251839 Cat. No. TO-521. 115V.1320W. AC Only. Westinghouse Mansfield Ohio Made in USA Manufactured Under One or More of the Following Patents: (patent numbers listed). Other Patents Pending." $35.00.

WESTINGHOUSE

late 1940s, 7⅛" high, chrome body with Bakelite handles, knob and base. Both handles are marked: "Westinghouse." Marked on the bottom: "J186345 Cat. No. To 71 115V 1000W Westinghouse Mansfield Ohio. Made in the USA Manufactured Under One or More of the Following Patents (several patent numbers listed). Other Patents Pending." $35.00.

TOASTERS

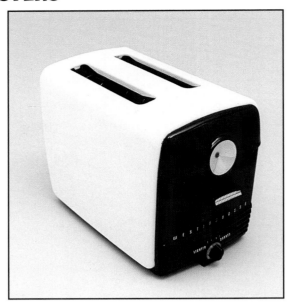

WESTINGHOUSE

Pop-Up, 1950s, 7¼" high, white baked-on enamel body with black hard plastic ends and base, light and dark heat control. Marked on the bottom: "Cat. No. 5421-W 115V 1320W A.C. Only. Westinghouse Mansfield Ohio. Made In USA." $75.00.

WESTINGHOUSE

Pop-Up Toaster, late 1940s, 7⅛" high, chrome body with black Bakelite handles, knobs, and base. Marked on the bottom: "K2382,57, 11655, 38885 Cat. No. TO-91. 115V 1000W Westinghouse Mansfield, Ohio Made in USA Manufactured Under One Or More of the Following Patents. 2,253,37; 2,2674,093; 2,274,724; 2,302,131; 2,336,696; 2,362,836; 2,407,984; 2,389,927. DES 150,134 Other Patents Pending." One of the interesting features I find in a number of ads on toasters is the advertising for a special Christmas gift, such as: "Give Mom and everyone on your Christmas list a special gift that can be enjoyed all year." It is ironic that today's toaster collectors would be ecstatic to find that special toaster they have been searching for under *their* Christmas trees. $35.00.

WESTINGHOUSE

Pop-Up Toaster, late 1940s, 7¼" high, fancy embossed chrome body with fancy embossed Bakelite handles, knobs and base, light and dark heat control. Marked on the bottom: "J228399 Cat. No. TO-71. 115V 1000W Westinghouse Mansfield Ohio, Made in the USA. Manufactured Under One or More of the Following Patents (patent numbers listed). Other Patents Pending." $40.00.

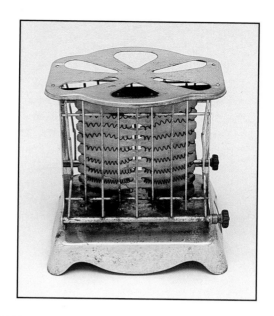

WESTINGHOUSE

Turnover, mid 1917 – 1924, 6⅞" high, nickel plated body with Bakelite handles, ceramic core with laced coil heating element, no heat control. Nameplate reads: "Turnover Toaster, Westinghouse Elec. & Manufacturing Company, A. Pittsburg Copeman Patents 5600 Volts 100-110 Style 231570 Amps 5.7." $75.00.

WESTINGHOUSE

Turnover, 1917 – 1924, 7" high, nickel plated body with Bakelite handles, fiber feet, off/on switch on cord, mica core heating element. Marked on the bottom: "Turnover Toasters. No. 284032A W WEP Volts 100-120 Watts 550 Lmp Patented 7-28-14, 8-25-14. Westinghouse E & M Co. Mansfield Works, Mansfield, Ohio." Note: Even though the three toasters on this page appear to be the same, there are a number of differences. The top cutout section of all three toasters serves as a warming rack for toast or a coffee pot. This style top is referred to as a "wheel top." $50.00.

WESTINGHOUSE

Turnover, 1917 – 1924, 7" high, nickel plated body with mica element, black Bakelite handles, fiber feet, no heat control. Nameplate reads: "Turnover Toaster W. Westinghouse Electric Copeman Patents." The first toaster to mechanically assist turning over the slices, untouched by human hands. $50.00.

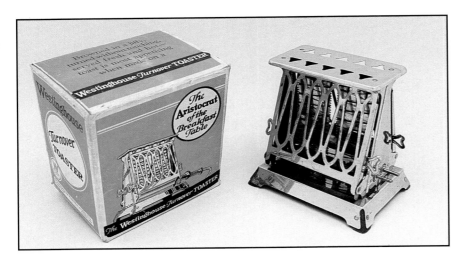

WESTINGHOUSE

Turnover, with original box, 1914 – 1920s, 7½" high, highly polished nickel body with cool metal handles and fiber feet. Marked on the bottom: "Westinghouse Turnover Toaster Cat.# TT-3 110V 550W Pat 7-28-14, 8-25-14 Westinghouse Elec. & Manufacturing Company, Mansfield Works Mansfield Ohio USA." $125.00 with original box.

WESTINGHOUSE

Turnover, early 1900s, 8" high, chrome plated body with black wooden handles and fiber feet, no heat control. Marked on the bottom: "Westinghouse Turnover Toaster Cat.# TDC-4 115V 550W Pat. 7-28-14, 8-25-14. Westinghouse Elec. & Manufacturing Company, Mansfield Works Mansfield Ohio, USA." $55.00.

WESTINGHOUSE

Turnover, 1930s, 7⅝" high, chrome body with black Bakelite front door pulls, wafer feet, no heat control. Marked on the bottom: "Westinghouse Turnover Toaster Cat.# 77C-94. 115V 550W Pat. 7-28-14, 8-25-14 Westinghouse Elec. & Manufacturing Company, Mansfield Works Mansfield Ohio, USA." $55.00.

WESTINGHOUSE

Turnover, 1920s, 7⅝" high, chrome plated body with fiber handles and feet. Marked on the bottom: "Westinghouse Turnover Toaster Cat.# TAC-3 110V 550W Pat. 7-28-14, 8-26-14 Westinghouse Elec. & Manufacturing Company, Mansfield Works Mansfield Ohio USA." $125.00.

WESTINGHOUSE

Turnover, shown in open position. Note how the one-piece formed doors make the complete upper section of the toaster body. The doors rest against an inner wire frame that holds the mica heating element. No heat control. This is a very unique toaster in design and is one of my favorites. $125.00.

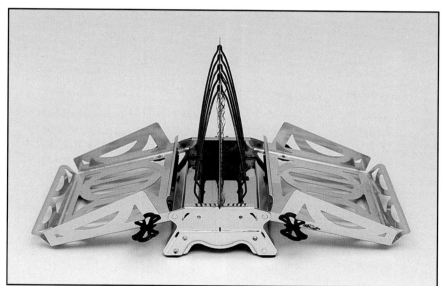

WESTINGHOUSE

Turnover, 1930s, 7⅝" high, chrome plated body with wooden handles and fiber feet. Marked on the bottom: "Westinghouse Turnover Toaster Cat.# TTC-53 110V 550W Pat. 7-28-14, 8-25-14 Westinghouse Elec. & Manufacturing Company, Mansfield Works Mansfield Ohio USA." $45.00.

WESTINGHOUSE

Turnover, 1920s, 7½" high, chrome plated body with fiber handles and feet, no heat control. Marked on the bottom: "Westinghouse Turnover Toaster Cat.# TTC-33 110V 550W Pat. 7-28-14, 8-25-14 Westinghouse Elec. & Manufacturing Company, Mansfield Works Mansfield Ohio USA." $45.00.

WESTINGHOUSE

Turnover, 1930s, 7¼" high, chrome body with Bakelite handles and wafer feet, mica heating element. Marked on the bottom: "Westinghouse Turnover Toaster Cat.# TE-4. 115V 400W Made in USA Westinghouse Elec. & Manufacturing Company, Mansfield Works Mansfield Ohio USA." $30.00.

WHITE CROSS

late 1930s, 7⅛" high, chrome plated body with black Bakelite handles and feet, no heat control. Marked on the bottom: "White Cross National Stamping & Elec Wks. Chicago USA 115V Model 327 575W." The handle on the right is stationary, and the left handle when raised brings toast rack up to place bread in. The toast rack then lowers for toasting, and the lever must again be pushed up to remove the toast manually. $45.00.

WHITE CROSS
1940s, 7½" high, chrome body with brown Bakelite handles and base. Marked on the bottom: "White Cross National Stamping and Elec. Wks. Made in USA Chicago 115V AC Only 850 W." $40.00.

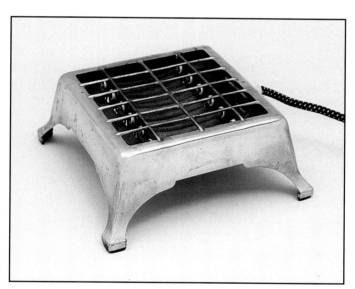

WILWEAR STOVE
early 1900s, 3" high, nickel plated body with attached black wafer type feet, heating element is laced open spring-coil, no heat control. Bottom is marked "4-5A - 110V. Patents Pending Wilwear Utility Stove. Novelty Mfg. Co. Waterbury, Conn. USA." $20.00

WOLFF
Visible Toaster, 1930s, 4⅜" high, stove top toaster which is non-electric, pierced tin bottom, fold-up wire tops. Toast four slices at one time. Marked: "Wolff Visible Toaster Pat. Sept. 21-20." This toaster was made by Wolff Appliance Corp. 42-33 Twelfth Street Long Island City, New York, USA. Note: The pamphlet advertises this special limited offer: "This coupon and 15 cents entitles you to one of these hand folding gas toasters if presented at our East Avenue show rooms before December 31, 1935." Similar toasters are still being made. $20.00.

UNMARKED TOASTERS

Single Sandwich, unmarked, 1930s, 4⅜" high, green enameled body with black Bakelite handle, wafer feet. One of the metal arms on the back side that supports the cover when raised for toasting plain and three decker sandwiches is marked: "Pat. pend." $75.00.

Toaster, unmarked, late 1930s, 7⅜" high, chrome finish with black Bakelite carrying handles, vertical torpedo-shaped handles, flip-over doors turn toast. Marked on the bottom: "Series 687 570 Watts 120 Volts AC-DC Seel-USA." Note: Even though this toaster is not marked with a manufacturer, I believe it is a product of the Son-Chief Electrics Inc. of Winsted, Connecticut USA. because it resembles the Magic Maid toaster made by the same company. $20.00.

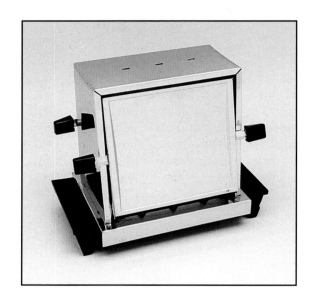

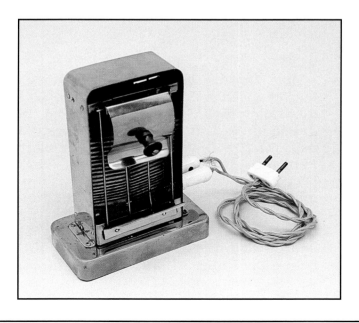

Toaster, unmarked, early 1900s, 6⅝" high, brass plated body. Marked on the right side: "110V 4A". This toaster holds ½ slice on each side. The free-hanging toast door with black wooden knob is pulled up and out to place bread against the heating elements. This type toaster is referred to as a "gravity-operated pincher." Note: The separated two prong white porcelain plug, and also the white porcelain plug on the end. The manufacturer's name and make are not present on this toaster. I believe this toaster is of foreign origin, even though the free-hanging toast door resembles a toaster made by an American company around 1915. $250.00 with original porcelain plug cord.

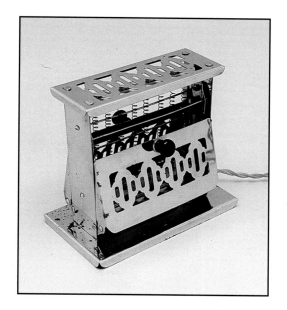

Toaster, name and manufacturer unmarked, 1920s, 6⅜" high. Marked on bottom: "Volts 110 Watts 450". Note: I believe this could be a product of the Manning-Bowman & Co., due to the type of decorative piercing on the doors and top of the toaster. The underside of the base has the electric cord attachment exposed. The small doors leave part of the element exposed, and could cause electrical shock when the door is opened to remove toast. $50.00.

Toaster, unmarked name and manufacturer, early 1900s, 6½" high, chrome plated with black wooden door pull. The open spring-coil heating element is laced through a ceramic core on the top and bottom section of the toaster. Marked on the bottom: "Volts 110 - Watts 450." Note: The size of the pierced doors, and that they only cover about ¾ of the heating element. I think this is a Manning-Bowman & Co. toaster. When I first saw this toaster, I thought it had part of the base missing, because it did not look in proportion to me. Since then I have seen several like it. $55.00.

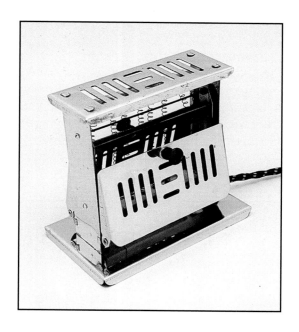

Toaster, unmarked, 1920s, 6⅝" high, nickel plated body with painted black enamel base and wooden handles, mica heating element, no heat control. $30.00.

Toaster, unmarked, 1920s, 7" high, nickel plated body with black wooden handles, molded metal base feet, no heat control. Coil wire heating element is laced over a top and bottom asbestos coated rod. Bottom section is laced over the bottom rod twice rather than once like the lacing commonly seen. $30.00.

Toaster, unmarked, 1920s, 7⅛" high, nickel plated body with wood handles and molded feet, no heat control, coil wire heating element is laced over a top and bottom ceramic rod. Bottom section is unusual in that it is laced twice over the ceramic rod rather than once like the usual lacing. $35.00.

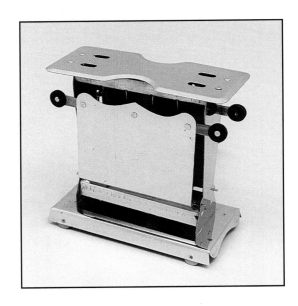

Toaster, unmarked, 1930s, 6¾" high, chrome body with brown wooden knobs and feet, mica heating element w/no controlled heat, fancy perforated top. $30.00.

Toaster, unmarked, late 1920s, 7" high, chrome body with scalloping on door tops and base sides, wafer style door pulls, and feet. $30.00.

Toaster, unmarked, 1930s, 6⅞" high, nickel plated doors with rough textured black body, metal feet, Bakelite turning knob. Both doors are opened by manually turning the knob on the right side towards you. Both doors close when you turn the knob away from you. $35.00.

Toaster, unmarked, 1930s, 7⅛" high, chrome body with wafer handles, mica heating element, no heat control. $35.00.

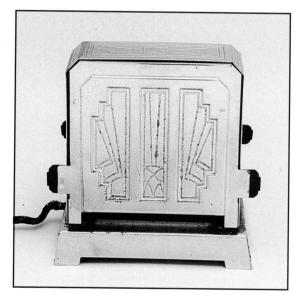

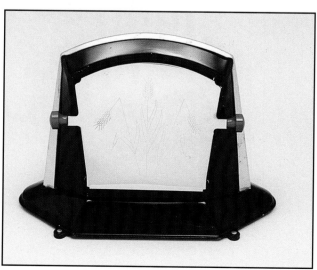

Toaster, unmarked, late 1930s, 8¼" high, chrome plated doors and trim with painted black enamel sides and base, red Bakelite handles and fiber feet, paneled mica heating elements. $85.00.

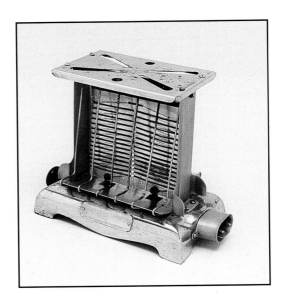

Toaster, unmarked, early 1900s, 7" high, nickel plated body with black wooden carry handle, mica heating element, no heat control or moving parts. Bread rests on wire structure for toasting. Bread has to be turned manually. On the bottom of the wire structure is an attached rounded tray to catch the crumbs and also for easier cleaning. This toaster also has a weighted bottom to keep it stabilized while in use. $110.00.

Toaster, unmarked, electric, early 1900s. 6¼" high. The body of this toaster is charcoal gray and white medium mottled graniteware. Fancy perforated metal toast center that is removable (see photo below). The wire toast holder on each side has a pottery type green knob that holds the bread against the perforated center. I believe this toaster was made in Germany, due to the color of graniteware used. $650.00.

Photo shows toaster above at right with perforated metal center removed, showing the very unusual ceramic and coil wound heating element. $650.00.

Toaster, unmarked, late 1930s, 7⅞" high, chrome body with black painted base, sides, and wooden handles. $30.00.

Toaster, unmarked, 1930s, 8" high, chrome doors and tops with black painted side, black Bakelite handles and attached tray base, no heat control. Note: Even though this toaster is unmarked, it could be a product of the Samson United Corp. Rochester, N.Y. $55.00.

Toaster, unmarked, early 1900s, 6¾" high, nickel plated body with wire handles and wooden feet, no heat control, horizontal laced coil heating element. $55.00.

Toaster, unmarked, stove-top, non-electric, early 1900s, 5¼" high, heavy metal body with wire toast racks and perforated sides. $35.00.

Toaster-hotplate, unmarked, combination, late 1930s, 10¼" high, Heat is controlled by off-on switches on front of the unit. Toast has to be popped-up manually. $150.00.

TOASTER ACCESSORIES

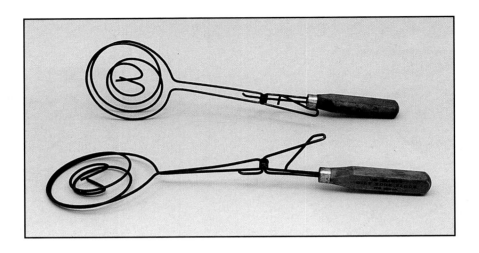

Top:
Advertising Toasting Fork, circa 1910, 15" long by 4¼", wire with wooden handle. Advertising on wooden handle reads: "For The Best Toast Use C. Edgar Lewis Bread Pottstown, PA." Note: This fork is more valuable because it tells the place it was manufactured. $75.00.

Bottom:
Advertising Toasting Fork, circa 1910, 15" long by 4¼", wire with wooden handle. Advertising on wooden handle reads: "Use Flory's Gilt Edge Flower For Bread." Note: When the wire thumb lift is pushed down, the section that holds the bread opens up for the bread to be placed in for toasting. $70.00.

Cookie Jar, toaster-shaped, 1950s, 7¾" high, made to represent the toasters of the 1940s. Body and cover are made of porcelain with a baked-on finish that is done to resemble chrome, black handles, base and lettering. Also note the glass piece on the front that represents the heat control light on the electric toaster. $75.00.

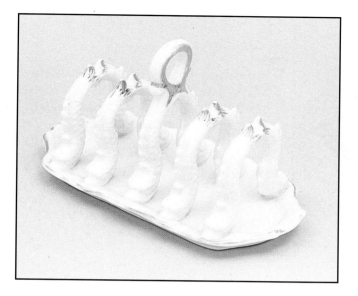

Dolphins Toast Rack, 1930s, 4⅞" high x 8¼" long x 4¼" wide. White porcelain decorated and trimmed in gold plate. Numbered on the bottom: "1010." $65.00.

Flat Top/Hotplate, 1920s, 3½" high x 6⅜" long x 5⅜" wide, body is nickel plated, laced coil heating element, no heat control, unmarked. The plug on the attached cord is designed to fit into a standard screw-in light bulb socket. Plug is marked "Pat. Appd. For." $15.00.

Lazy Susan serving set with toast rack, unmarked, 1940s. Tray is 11½" in diam. by 2¼" high. Includes four glass serving pieces with aluminum covers. $45.00.

Sandwich Grill, 1930s, 4½" high x 13½" long x 6½" wide, chrome body with fancy embossed top, black Bakelite handles and wafer feet. Marked on the bottom: "Waage Mfg. Co. Chicago Ill." $55.00.

Slice-A-Slice, 1940s – 1950s, 7⅝" high, chrome plated body with rubber feet. Marked on top: "Duncannon, PA Slice-A-Slice Pat. 2,172,538. 2,206,154." Box section reads: "Slice-A-Slice, Re-Slices ready-cut bread for attractive sandwiches." Note: The bread is placed inside the Slice-A-Slice, then closed and held by hand while using a knife to slice the bread. $20.00.

Combination Toast Rack with spoons and egg cups, late 1920s, 7" high, tray 7⅜" long x 5⅝" wide. Spoons marked "WM. A ROGERS A1." Bottom of tray numbered 47991. $95.00.

Toast Rack souvenir, 1930s, 4⅝" high x 7" long x 3⅝" wide, white porcelain body with gold trim. Decorated on each end with a scene from the "Southend Pier," pictured are three guns with bayonets standing upright. Marked on the bottom: "Made In Germany." $65.00.

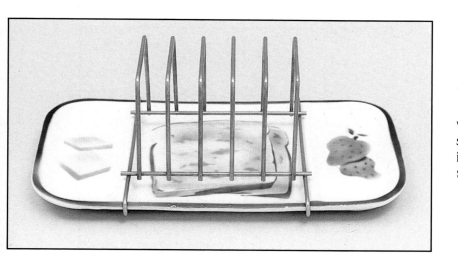

Toast Rack with attached metal rack, 1940s, 3⅜" high x 8¾" long x 4¾" wide. Porcelain body decorated with strawberries, toast, and butter. Design is trimmed in green. Unmarked. $50.00.

Toast Rack, late 1930s, 3" high x 7¼" long x 4" wide. Pearlized iridescent finish decorated with orange and black trim. Green, orange, and yellow decoration on each end. Marked: "Made In Japan." $55.00.

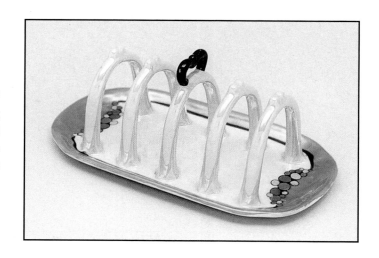

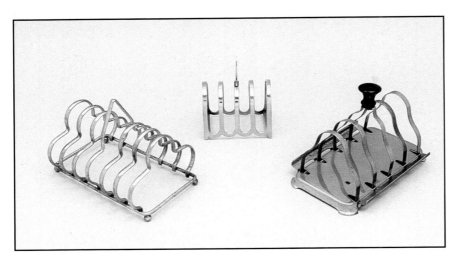

Left:
Toast Rack, 1940s, 4½" high x 6¼" long x 3⅜" wide, metal plated, unmarked. $25.00.

Center:
Toast Rack, 1930s, 4⅜" high x 3⅜" long x 2⅜" wide, metal with brass plate. Marked on the bottom: "E.P.N.S." $25.00.

Right:
Toast Rack, late 1910s, 4¾" high x 6¼" long x 4¼" wide, polished nickel plated steel with ebonized wooden handle. This rack is designed to fit snugly atop the gravity operated Royal Rochester toaster, shown elsewhere in this book. This removable toast rack makes an easy way to pass around toast. $75.00.

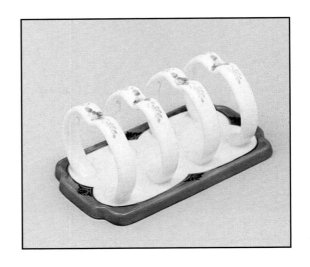

Toast Rack, late 1930s, 2¼" high x 5⅛" long x 2⅞" wide. White porcelain body decorated with pink roses and leaves. Trimmed in blue. Marked on the bottom: "M Japan." $55.00.

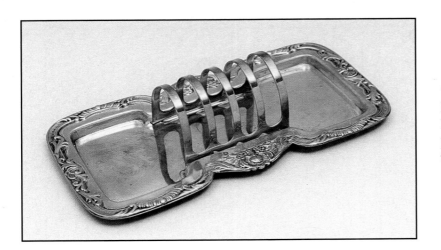

Toast Rack, 1930s. Marked on the bottom: "ART S CO SR-65." I believe this toast rack was silver plated and someone stripped off the plating. $45.00.

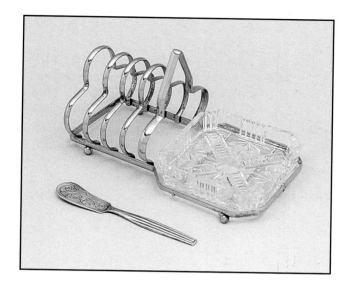

Toast Rack, late 1940s, 3 pieces, rack, fancy embossed butter knife, and pressed glass jelly dish. Toast rack unmarked, butter knife marked: "Sheffield Eng. Silver Plated." Jelly dish marked: "England." $65.00.

Left:
Toast Rack, late 1970s, 1¾" high, chrome finish. Marked on bottom: "W.M.F. Cromargan, Germany." $30.00.

Center:
Toast Rack, 2-piece, late 1980s, 2¾" high, unmarked, chrome plated. $20.00.

Right:
Toast Rack, 2-piece, late 1940s. Bottom section marked: "59 Oneida,¹⁸⁄₈ Japan Art Deco." $35.00.

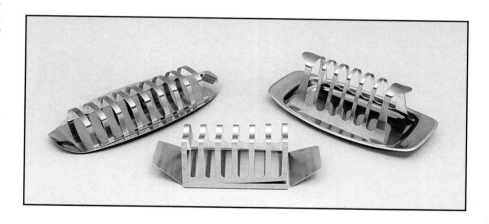

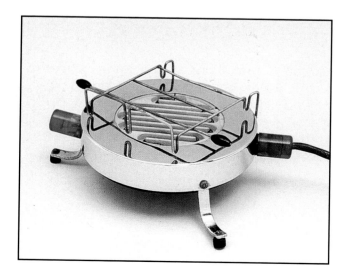

Toast Stove-Hotplate, unmarked, 1930s, 3⅞" high, chrome plated body with reddish-brown marbleized Bakelite carrying handles, black Bakelite knob and feet. The toast rack swings up and back so the unit can be used as a hotplate. $85.00.

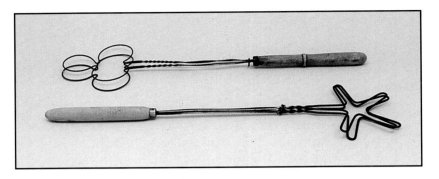

Top:
Toasting Fork, circa 1910, 19¼" long x 4½", three-leaf clover pattern, wire with wooden handle. Note: This toasting fork works in the same manner as the star-shaped one below. $55.00

Bottom:
Toasting Fork, circa 1910, 19" long by 5⅛", star shape, wire with wooden handle. Note: When the wire ring on the center of the toast fork is pushed back towards the wooden handle, the section that holds the bread for toasting opens up. $55.00.

Toastoy, (pictured from left to right), late 1920s – 1930s, 5" high, chrome body with fancy tulip type cut-outs on each door, wafer feet. Manufactured by The Excel Electric Co. Muncie, Indiana. U.S.A. Each door is embossed on lower inside edge: "Electric Excel Toastoy Excel." The heat element is Nichrome 150 Watt. This toaster holds ½ slice of bread on each side. The doors are operated manually. Notice the all metal doors, and how they would more than likely burn your child's fingers when in operation. $225.00 with original box. $175.00 without box.

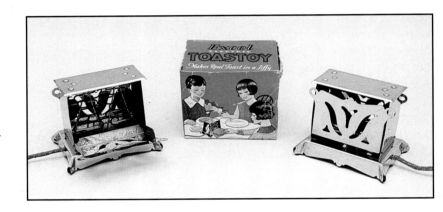

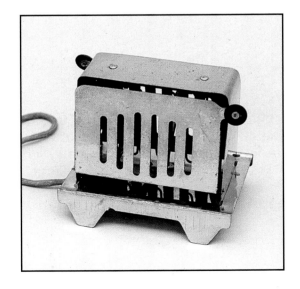

Toy Toaster, late 1930s, 4½" high, chrome body with wafer handles. Marked on the bottom: "Lady Junior." Vertically laced open spring-coil heating element. No heat control, each door is operated manually, maker unknown. $65.00.

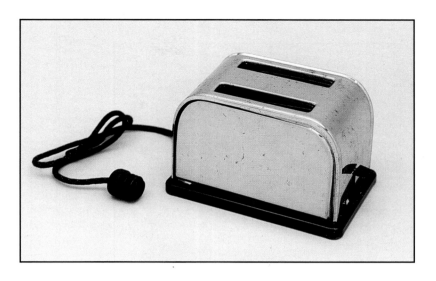

Toy Toaster, electric, unmarked, late 1930s, 5⅝" high, chrome body with black base and applied top decoration. Wafer handles, vertically laced open spring-coil heating element, no heat control, each door is operated manually. Note: I also believe this toaster is another version of the Lady Junior. Maker unknown. $65.00.

Toy Toaster, non-electric, late 1940s, 3½" high, chrome body with black painted base, non-electric cord and plug. Marked on the bottom: "Northwestern Products St. Louis, Made in the USA." $25.00.

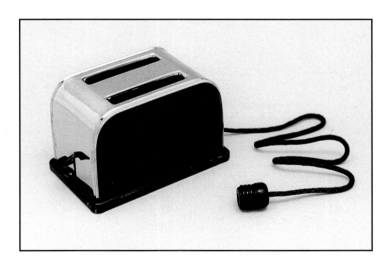

Toy Toaster, non-electric, 1970s, 5" high, tin body with painted decorated sides and plastic base. Marked on lower section of toaster: "435KC177 The Ohio Art Company, Bryan Ohio 43506, USA." When lever on the side is pushed down, bread is lowered into the toaster, and when lever is pushed sideways, bread pops up. $25.00.

Toy Toaster, non-electric, late 1940s, 3½" high, chrome body with black painted sides and base, non electric cord and plug, unmarked. Each toast basket holds ½ slice of bread. Bread is lowered into the toaster when lever on the side is pushed down and locked into a groove made in the toaster body. Note: Even though this toy toaster is unmarked, I believe it is a product of the Northwest Products St. Louis. $25.00.

Toy Toaster, non-electric, 1970s, 5" high, tin body with painted decorated sides and plastic base. Marked on lower section of toaster: "421E173." $20.00.

Toy Toaster, unmarked, late 1950s, 5" high, tin body with red enamel painted sides and black decorations, black plastic handles and attached base. Note: When button on the left side is pushed down, a wind-up spring mechanism that gives the sound effect of a timer on a real toaster pushes the "bread" up and out of the toaster. $25.00.

Toy Toaster, Sunnie Miss, 1970s, non-electric, 5" high, tin body with painted decorated sides and plastic base. Marked on the lower section of the toaster: "435B177 The Ohio Art Company, Bryan, Ohio 43506 U.S.A. Lite and Dark." $25.00.

Wedgewood Toast Rack, 1930s, 2¼" high x 7¼" long x 3⅜" wide. Decorated with pattern and marked on the bottom: "Covent Garden of Entrucia & Barlaston Wedgewood Made in England 11G60 Wedgewood." $65.00.

CATALOG REPRINTS

Advertisement for the Edicraft Speed Toaster, late 1920s tells how the Edicraft Speed Toaster works. $20.00.

Page from a 1939 Toastwell Electric Company, St. Louis, Missouri, catalog. Catalog price $75.00.

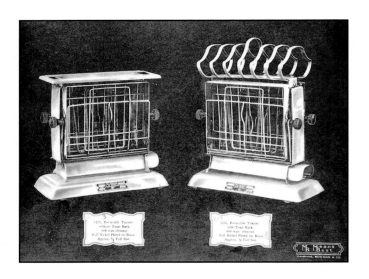

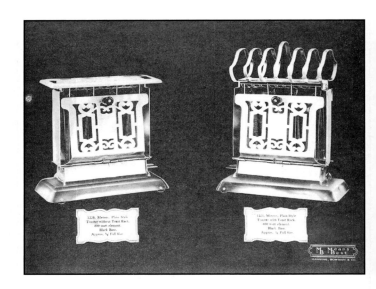

Page from late 1920s Manning-Bowman & Company, Meriden, Conn. catalog. Shows the 1225 Reversible Toaster without the toast rack on the left; on the right is the 1226 Reversible toaster with the toast rack. Both toasters have a 600 watt element. Finish is full nickel plated on brass. Catalog price $85.00.

Page from late 1920s Manning-Bowman catalog. Showing the 1220 Meteor plain style toaster without toast rack on the left, and on the right, the 1221 with the toast rack. Both toasters have a 600 watt element. Catalog price $85.00.

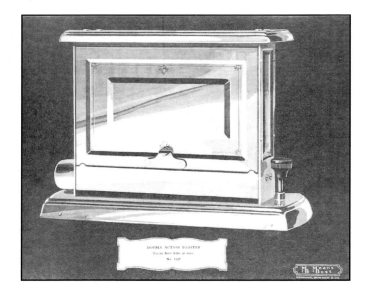

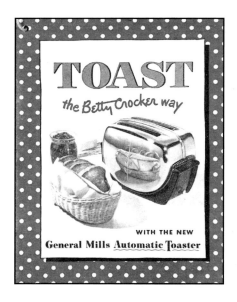

Page from 1920s Manning-Bowman & Company catalog. Showing the 1227 double action toaster. Toasts both sides at once. Catalog price $85.00.

1949 General Mills Booklet, 5½" x 4¼". Describes the use and care of the General Mills Automatic toaster and its outstanding features, as well as recipes for toast treats. $25.00.

Advertisement for the 1937 Toastmaster Deluxe Hospitality Tray set. Note: This is one of the sets offered for the 1937 Christmas trade ad. $20.00.

Advertisement for the 1931 one-slice Toastmaster Toaster, stating that the one- slice Toastmaster toaster is faster than most two-slice toasters. $20.00.

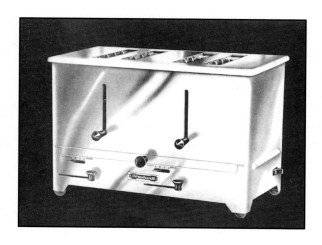

Page from a 1930 Utility Electrical Appliances catalog, showing the 4-slice automatic Toastwell Toaster, with separate "Micro Control" for each two-slice section. Toasts to any desired degree, then stops toasting — keeps toast hot and tasty until ready to serve. This toaster was advertised to toast 240 slices per hour. Catalog price $75.00.

TURN-EASY TOASTER CHEVALIER PATTERN

A striking new toaster, designed to harmonize with other Chevalier Pattern Electric Appliances. Here is the same Heavy Matched Walnut Knobs, the same Brilliant Non-Tarnishing Chromium, the same scheme of decoration. Opening the toast rack turns the toast. Takes slice of bread 5 x 4¾ inches. Equipped with one piece heat conserving door. An efficient economical toaster that is built to last a lifetime.

No. E8612   Weight packed 3½ lbs.   Watts 625

TURN-EASY TOASTER HEPPLE-WHITE PATTERN

A toaster that combines the beauty of design characteristic of the Hepple-White era with the practical features demanded in a toaster of today. All exposed metal plated with Gleaming Chromium, the finish that never tarnishes. Knobs, Handles and Feet are of durable heat-proof Ivory Casein, a composition that closely resembles genuine ivory. Accommodates bread any size up to 5 x 4¾ inches and quickly toasts it to a beautiful golden brown.

No. E7712   Weight packed 3½ lbs.   Watts 625

TURN-EASY TOASTER ELITE PATTERN

A striking new toaster of the ever popular Turn-Easy Type. Base and Top are finished with Black Heat-Resisting Enamel. Solid Metal Doors and Sides are plated with Gleaming Non-Tarnishing Chromium. Opening toast rack turns the toast. Black Knobs and Feet give artistic touch. A toaster that combines beauty, efficiency, durability and ease of operation with moderate price.

No. E3612   Weight packed 3 lbs.   Watts 625

UNIVERSAL Electric Toasters

AUTOMATIC TOASTER MODERNE PATTERN

Makes perfect toast without watching — light, medium or dark as desired. Toasts both sides of two slices 5 x 4¼ in. at a time. Black Composition Handles and Soft Rubber Feet. Chromium Plated. Six foot cord. Watts 800.

No. E7822
Weight packed, 6¾ lbs.

DEVONSHIRE PATTERN BELL SIGNAL TOASTER

Automatically rings the bell when toast is ready and switches the current from a toasting heat to a low serving heat. Ideal for "Melba" toast. Toasts bread 5 x 4¼ in. Mahogany Composition Handles and Feet. Chromium Plated. Six foot cord. Watts 800.

No. E2122
Weight packed, 5½ lbs.   For A. C. only

DOUBLE-QUICK OVEN TOASTER

Ideal for large families. Toasts both sides of two slices 5 x 4¼ in. at a time. Black Composition Handles. Chromium Plated. Six foot cord. Watts 800.

No. E7722
Weight packed, 4½ lbs.

DEVONSHIRE PATTERN MUFFIN AND BREAD TOASTER

The charming motif of this pattern is taken from the Adam design which was so popular during the early 18th Century. Mahogany Composition Trim. Toasts bread 5 x 4¾ in. Its specially designed bread rack also holds muffins. Chromium Plated. Six foot cord. Watts 525.

No. E221
Weight packed, 3¼ lbs.

1937 catalog page from the "Reprinted" Universal Electrical Appliance catalog showing three of the Turn Easy toasters. Catalog with price list $75.00.

1940 catalog page from the Revised Edition Universal Electrical Appliance catalog, No. 1413. Landers, Frary, & Clark. New Britain, Conn. Catalog price $75.00.

Catalog page from the 1937 "Reprinted" Universal Electrical Appliances catalog showing the "Moderne Pattern" Automatic Toaster. Stating: "The finest ever made by Universal." Catalog with price list $75.00.

UNIVERSAL
Electric Toasters

CORONET PATTERN

Opening the toast rack turns the toast. Toasts bread 5 x 4¾ in. Black Bakelite Ends, Feet and Knobs. Chromium Plated with decorative "Platina" panel. Six foot cord. Watts 525.

No. E1321

Weight packed, 3 lbs.

MAYFAIR PATTERN

Opening the toast rack turns the toast. Toasts bread 5 x 4¾ in. Chestnut Brown Bakelite Ends, Feet and Knobs. Chromium Plated. Six foot cord. Watts 525.

No. E1221

Weight packed, 3 lbs.

STREAMLINED PATTERN

Opening the toast rack turns the toast. Toasts bread 5 x 4¾ in. Walnut Knobs. Chromium Plated. Six foot cord. Watts 625.

No. E8212

Weight packed, 3½ lbs.

No. 8212

SOUTHINGTON PATTERN

Opening the toast rack turns the toast. Toasts bread 5 x 4¾ in. Black Composition Knobs and Feet. Chromium Plated. Six foot cord. Watts 550.

No. E7211

Weight packed, 3 lbs.

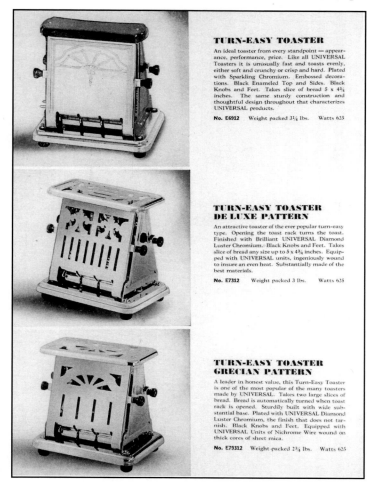

TURN-EASY TOASTER

An ideal toaster from every standpoint — appearance, performance, price. Like all UNIVERSAL Toasters it is unusually fast and toasts evenly, either soft and crunchy or crisp and hard. Plated with Sparkling Chromium. Embossed decorations. Black Enameled Top and Sides. Black Knobs and Feet. Takes slice of bread 5 x 4¾ inches. The same sturdy construction and thoughtful design throughout that characterizes UNIVERSAL products.

No. E6912   Weight packed 3¼ lbs.   Watts 625

TURN-EASY TOASTER DE LUXE PATTERN

An attractive toaster of the ever popular turn-easy type. Opening the toast rack turns the toast. Finished with Brilliant UNIVERSAL Diamond Luster Chromium. Black Knobs and Feet. Takes slice of bread any size up to 5 x 4¾ inches. Equipped with UNIVERSAL units, ingeniously wound to insure an even heat. Substantially made of the best materials.

No. E7312   Weight packed 3 lbs.   Watts 625

TURN-EASY TOASTER GRECIAN PATTERN

A leader in honest value, this Turn-Easy Toaster is one of the most popular of the many toasters made by UNIVERSAL. Takes two large slices of bread. Bread is automatically turned when toast rack is opened. Sturdily built with wide substantial base. Plated with UNIVERSAL Diamond Luster Chromium, the finish that does not tarnish. Black Knobs and Feet. Equipped with UNIVERSAL Units of Nichrome Wire wound on thick cores of sheet mica.

No. E79312   Weight packed 2¾ lbs.   Watts 625

1940 catalog page from the Revised Edition Universal Electrical Appliance catalog, No. 1413. Landers, Frary, & Clark, New Britain, Conn. Catalog price $75.00.

1937 catalog page from the "Reprinted" Universal Electrical appliance catalog showing three of the Turn Easy toasters. Catalog with price list $75.00.

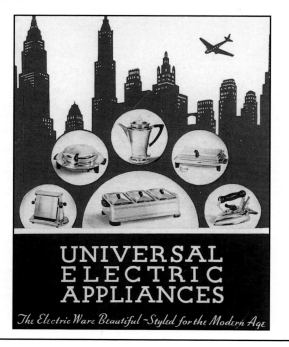

1937 "Reprinted" Universal Electric Appliances catalog including price list. Catalog with price list $75.00.

DOUBLE QUICK
OVEN TOASTER
BEAUMONDE PATTERN

Toasts both sides of two slices at a time. Requires no more space than the average table toaster. Plated with Non-Tarnishing Chromium. Top and Base are Enameled with Glistening Black. Handles are Black Bakelite. Feet are Heat Resisting Fibre. A toaster designed in harmony with other Electric Appliances of the Beautiful Beaumonde Pattern. Takes slice of bread 4 x 4¾ inches. Just the thing for families that demand extra capacity, and, ideal too, where hard usage demands sturdiness and durability.

No. E6722   Weight packed 4¾ lbs.   Watts 500

SNACK SET

In one complete unit the Hospitality Tray contains everything needed for serving a variety of canapes, appetizers and toasted sandwiches. The compartments of its glass container may be quickly filled with an assortment of jams, jellies, olives, pickles or sliced meats in an assortment large enough to suit the taste of every guest. Consists of No. E6722 Oven Toaster, shown above, together with a Walnut Tray, 24½ x 15½ inches, that will not warp or crack and that may be washed with soap and hot water. Five-Compartment Crystal Clear Glass Dish, 6¼ x 14½ inches, Walnut Cutting Block, 4¾ x 14¼ inches, Cutting Knife with seven inch Stainless Steel Blade and Ivory Grained Handle.

No. E86722   Tray, Glass Dish, Cutting Block and Knife packed in a carton. Toaster packed in separate carton. Weight of each package respectively 9¼ and 4¾ pounds.

1930s catalog page from the Universal Electrical Appliance catalog. Landers, Frary, & Clark. New Britain, Conn. Showing the No. E6722 Double Quick Oven Toaster in the "Beaumonde Pattern." Also shows how it's used with the Snack Set. Catalog price $75.00.

1937 catalog page from the "Reprinted" Universal Electrical Appliance Catalog. Catalog with price list $75.00.

TURN-EASY TOASTER
OLD ENGLISH PATTERN

A Toaster that fills every need for present day serving. All metal plated with durable Non-Tarnishing Chromium. Equipped with the specially wound UNIVERSAL Unit of Nichrome Wire that has made famous all UNIVERSAL Toasters. Ivory Casein Knobs and Feet. Decorative treatment is classic Old English. An appointment that will add to the grace and beauty of the most discriminating table-ware.

No. E7812   Weight packed 3 lbs.   Watts 625

TURN-EASY TOASTER

Fast becoming a leader in the field, this new toaster offers advanced design, handsome finish and efficient service. It is completely plated with UNIVERSAL Diamond Lüster Chromium, is equipped with fast even-toasting UNIVERSAL Units, takes a slice of bread as large as 5 x 4¾ inches and is built with the care that has made famous the name "UNIVERSAL". Its sturdiness makes it an ideal toaster for those families that serve toast every day in the year.

No. E7912   Weight packed 3¼ lbs.   Watts 625

TURN-EASY TOASTER
WALNUT HILL PATTERN

Decorated with the Walnut Hill Motif, this Turn-Easy Toaster is another member of this UNIVERSAL group of matched appliances. Brilliant, Tarnish-proof Chromium and Solid Walnut Handles. Here also is the usual UNIVERSAL high quality of material and construction. Quickly toasts bread of any size up to 5 x 4¾ in.

No. W8312   Weight packed 3½ lbs.   Watts 625

56 FARBERWARE

Farberware Serving Trays

Solid Brass, Heavy Gauge, is the base metal used in the manufacture of Farberware. This quality metal is Nickel Plated and then Chromium Plated—producing a permanent, rich, bright finish that will not tarnish

These handy Serving Trays are a necessity in every home. Useful for—

HOLDING A TOASTER
SERVING DRINKS
SERVING SNACKS
SERVING SANDWICHES
MADE FOR EVERYDAY SERVING

No. 6112—CHROMIUM PLATED SERVING TRAY.

No. 6110—CHROMIUM PLATED SERVING TRAY.
Length 12½", width 8"

No. 6321—CHROMIUM PLATED SERVING TRAY.
Made of heavy gauge solid brass. Length 13½", width 10½".

No. 6183—CHROMIUM PLATED SERVING TRAY

No. 6333—WALNUT PLYWOOD TRAY WITH CHROMIUM HANDLES—Liquor and Stain proof. Strong construction. Length 20", width 12".

No. 6118—CHROMIUM PLATED SERVING TRAY.
Length 18½", width 12".
No. 6111—Same as above but smaller.
Length 16", width 11½".

◄ DON'T ACCEPT SUBSTITUTES—DEMAND GENUINE FARBERWARE ►

Catalog page from the late 1930s. S. W. Farber Inc. Brooklyn, N.Y. Catalog. Features serving trays. Catalog price $75.00.

Catalog page from the 1930 – 1931 Simplex Division Edison General Electric Appliance Co. Inc. catalog. Showing the Deluxe Toaster No. 819T35 with the chrome plate finish and lifting handles. Price in the 1930 – 1931 catalog at $6.50, compared to the Toast Turner Toaster No. 816T26 with the highly polished nickel finish and no lift handle, priced at $5.00. Catalog with price list $75.00.

Chromeplate

DE LUXE TOASTER
No. 819T35

WE PREDICT that this high grade toaster will outsell any other toaster of equal price. It has five most desirable features that make selling easy.

1—**Tarnish-Proof Chromeplate Finish**—always bright and beautiful—will not tarnish or discolor with use.

2—**Artistic Calmold Lifting Handles.** Always cool. The user can lift the toaster and move it about, even with the current turned on.

3—**Highly Attractive Appearance**—the graceful, artistic design and ornamental piercing on top and sides appeal to the most particular purchaser.

4—**Toast-Turner Basket Sides**—toast is turned automatically when sides are lowered. Basket sides keep toast warm after current is turned off.

5—**Durable Glowing Coil Heating Element**—toasts the bread quickly and evenly. Gives years of service.

Toasts two large slices. Costs little to operate.

Gleaming, Tarnish-Proof Chromeplate Finish
Decorative Pierced Top and Sides
Calmold, Cool Lifting Handles
Cool Metal Handles to raise and lower sides

Calorite Heating Element
Non-Scratching Fibre Feet
Toast-Turner Basket Sides
Red and Black Silk Cord
Miniature Detachable Plug

Watts—660
Voltages—105, 115, 125
Standard Pkg.—3
Standard Shipt.—12
Ship. Weight—4½ Lbs.

TOAST-TURNER TOASTER
No. 816T26

FOR several years this toaster has been one of the fastest selling appliances in the famous Simplex line. No wonder its popularity has been so great—it's one of the most attractive table appliances on the market—it's well made throughout—toasts two large slices and turns the toast when sides are lowered. But, most important of all—its an exceptional value! Compare it with other toasters of similar price.

This moderately priced toaster is similar in design and construction to No. 819T35, above, except that it is finished in highly polished Nickel and is not equipped with lifting handles. The glowing coil heating element is of durable Calorite (best grade Nickel-Chromium Alloy wire). You can depend on this toaster to give years of satisfactory service.

Highly Polished Nickel Finish
Decorative Pierced Top and Sides
Correctly Spaced, Durable Calorite Heating Element
Cool Metal Handles

"Toast-Turner" Basket Sides
Non-Scratching Fibre Feet
Standard Simplex Green and Gray Cord
Miniature Detachable Plug

Watts—660
Voltages—105, 115, 125
Standard Package—3
Standard Shipt.—12
Shipping Weight—4½ Lbs.

ROYAL · ROCHESTER

SIGNAL CONTROL TWO SLICE TOASTER
The ARISTOCRAT

This is a beautiful, stylish, up-to-date toaster. Finished entirely in lustrous, non-tarnishing chrome. Beautiful pierced and embossed design. New one-piece construction. It tells you when the toast is done. That's what you want to know. Simply set for the degree of brownness you prefer and when one side of bread is toasted (the signal bell tells you when), just lower the doors and bread turns automatically. Raise doors ... set Signal Control lever ... and when the other side is perfectly toasted the signal bell rings. That's your signal to take out two pieces of golden, evenly browned toast.

No. 13370—List Price.............$5.95

The EMBASSY

This is one of the most beautiful toasters in America. Finished in gleaming, non-tarnishing chromium. Attractive embossed decoration. Equipped with genuine mica-core heating element. Long detachable cord. The Tray has jet black hard-baked enamel center while rim is finished in highly polished chromium.

No. 13970—List Price....$3.95
No. 22500 Tray—List Price$1.00

SIGNAL CONTROL TWO SLICE TOASTER
The AUTOCRAT

This toaster is the most outstanding value on the market today. Finished in heavily plated chrome and jet black. Chrome sides with black frame. The black is hard baked enamel affected by neither heat nor water. Attractive pierced and embossed design. New one piece construction. Genuine mica-core heating element. Assures perfect, evenly browned, crisp toast always. The signal tells you when the bread is perfectly toasted. Equipped with long detachable cord. Four cool turning knobs. Non-scratching feet. Concealed terminals.

No. 13400—List Price.............$4.95

The DELUXE

Finished in lustrous chrome and black chrome sides and black frame. This combination is the newest and most acceptable trend in modern table ware. And this toaster is an exceptionally fast seller. Attractive pierced and embossed design. Genuine mica-core element. Long detachable cord.

No. 13300—List Price.............$3.50

THE TRIUMPH

Finished with jet black, hard baked enamel frame ... and lustrous chromium doors. Makes two slices of toast. Genuine mica-core heating element. Four cool turning handles. Turn-over feature ... just lower doors and toast turns automatically. Complete with cord. Price to create volume and profits.

No. 13330—List Price $2.95

The PATRICIAN with SIGNAL-CONTROL
The VANITY without SIGNAL-CONTROL

Finished in lustrous chrome with jet black vertical inlays. Accurately designed full floating mica element guarantees uniform toast always. Four cool turning knobs. Non-scratching feet. Complete with long detachable cord.

No. 13520—With Signal-Control.........$5.95
No. 13420—With-out Signal-Control......$3.95

THE LENOX

Finished entirely in gleaming non-tarnishing chromium. Toasts two slices of bread. Turn-over feature. Four cool turning knobs. Non-scratching fibre feet. Genuine mica-core element. Complete with cord, priced for quantity sales and a handsome profit.

No. 13340—List Price $3.25

Page from the 1936 Royal Rochester Electric Appliances and Table Utilities, Robeson Corp. catalog. Showing a number of the Royal Rochester toasters. Catalog with price list $75.00.

Page from the 1930 – 1931 Simplex Division Edison General Electric Appliance Co., Inc. catalog. Showing the Simplex Toaster No. 816T34 with the decorative pierced non-turnover basket sides. Catalog with price list $75.00.

Simplex

SIMPLEX TOASTER
No. 816T34

HIGH quality at an unusually low price. This new Simplex toaster was designed especially to meet the popular demand for an attractive, well made toaster, priced to suit the purse of moderate means.

Before placing this toaster on the market we gave it some severe tests in our laboratory—then we placed a number of models in homes of both large and small families to receive the judgment of modern housewives. The laboratory tests proved that it is remarkably fast in operation, durable and economical. The housewives informed us that it makes perfect toast—that it is easy to use—satisfactory in every way.

A great value—sturdy, dependable, economical!

Polished Nickel Finish	Cool Metal Handles	Voltages—105, 115, 125
Decorative Pierced, Non-Turnover	Non-Scratching Fibre Feet	Standard Package—3
Basket Sides	Attached, Red and Black Cord	Standard Shipt.—12
Durable Heating	Watts—660	Ship. Weight—4½ Lbs.
Element of Chlorite.		

SIMPLEX IMMERSION HEATER
No. 815W36

QUICKLY heats any liquid in which it is immersed. Ideal for use in the home for warming baby's milk or heating water for shaving. Doctors, dentists, chemists and barbers will find it well suited to their needs. It is easy to use and may be attached to any convenient electric outlet. Large size; brings liquid to a boil in a few minutes.

Large Size— heats quickly

CALROD Heating Unit	Large Size—Heats Quickly
Practically Indestructible	Watts—500
Easy to Use	Volts—115,230,250
Economical	Shipping Wt.—1½ Lbs.
Cool Rest (See Illustration)	Standard Package—3
Attached Simplex Cord	Standard Shipt.—12

SIMPLEX IMMERSION HEATER
No. 813W36

Handy Small Size

SMALLER in size and capacity than No. 815W36 above. Fits any standard size tumbler. Heats quickly and economically. A convenient size for tourists. Equipped with CALROD, practically indestructible heating element. Moderately priced.

CALROD Heating Unit	Attached Simplex Cord
Practically Indestructible	Watts—300
Handy Small Size	Volts—115
Easy to Use	Shipping Wt.—1½ Lbs.
Economical	Standard Package—3
Attached Cool Rest	Standard Shipt.—12

[8]

TOASTERS

No. 1229

Nickel Plated, $8.00

Tip and Turn Toaster

Ornamented with chased design. Toasts a large slice of bread quickly. Has a large heating element.

No. 1227

Nickel Plated, $8.50

This model is equipped with a double heating unit and toasts both sides of the bread at the same time. Speedy in action.

No. 1225. $8.00

Reversible Door Type

Turn the knob on either side of the toast holder and you turn the toast. It cannot fail to operate and best of all you never touch the toast.

No. 1228. $6.00

Tip and Turn Toaster

A most popular style. Simply open and close the door to turn the toast. Never jams, never gets out of order.

Page from early 1930s Manning-Bowman Electric Appliances Catalog. Showing a number of their toasters. Catalog price $75.00.

Page from the 1935 Manning-Bowman Electric Appliances Catalog. Showing the No. 790, The Patrician (Harmony Pattern) toaster service. Note: The "Harmony" pattern is one of a number of patterns that have matched appliances, such as coffee pots, sugars and creamers, waffle irons, trays, glass dishes, etc. Catalog price $75.00.

The Patrician (HARMONY PATTERN) Toaster Service

Hail The "Patrician," a competent toaster service that smartly graces any serving table or breakfast table for it requires only a minimum of space—not big and bulky, but small and compact. Hostesses will delight in the "Patrician" because of its beauty, too—it is of the popular Harmony Pattern and all three units—toaster—tray—and crystal glass marmalade or jam dish nicely complement each other.

The toaster itself has the convenient "tip and turn" type all metal doors and an efficient nichrome wound mica heating element that toasts bread evenly and quickly. 18½" x 8" are the dimensions of the capable tray which is ideal for all serving. Both toaster and tray are finished in lustrous non-tarnishing chromium with serviceable bakelite trimmings of contrasting black. And—the crystal glass marmalade or jam dish will be the joy of every housewife for it has two compartments—it can be placed in the refrigerator when not in use. The glass dish, too, is daintily decorated with the Harmony Pattern border around the top edge. Truly the "Patrician" lives up to its name for it is the "deluxe" toaster and serving ensemble.

No. 790 Toaster Service
Code "Monad"

Watts 470

Standard Package 3

Shipping Weight 8 lbs.

[18]

L&H ELECTRICS TOASTER

No. 204 L&H Electrics Toaster

Height	...................7¼ in.	Volts	110-120
Width	...................7¼ in.	Watts	550
Depth	...................5¼ in.	Shipping Weight (3 Toasters)	...11 lbs.
Toasting Surface	...........4¾x5¾ in.	Code	...................Toastlore

DURABILITY and quick-toasting service are paramount in the construction of the L&H Electrics Toasters. Toast is turned automatically and efficiently. The heating element is so made that even distribution of heat assures evenly browned bread to the right degree of crispiness. The draft damper under the door prevents drafts from interfering during the process of toasting.

THIS toaster has a steel braced unit, damper-on-the-door feature and is the same size as Model No. 202 excepting that the bread reversing mechanism is in one piece. The handles are at the bottom of the doors. Each toaster equipped with cord and terminal plug and is wrapped in tissue paper, packed in a neat carton. The heavy nickel finish, highly polished, is durable and adds to its attractiveness.

Page from late 1920s A. J. Lindemann & Hoverson Co. Milwaukee, Wisconsin, Electrical Appliances catalog. Showing their No. 204 L&H Electrics toaster. This toaster has a "Steel Braced unit, with damper on the door feature." The bread reversing mechanism is in one piece and the handles are at the bottom of the doors. Catalog price $85.00.

Page from late 1920s A. J. Lindemann & Hoverson Co. Milwaukee, Wisconsin, Electrical Appliances Catalog. Showing their No. 202 L&H Electrics Turnsit Toaster. The "TURNSIT" mechanism reverses the toast automatically each time the door is dropped. The extra large top is for keeping toast warm. Catalog price $85.00.

L&H ELECTRICS TOASTER

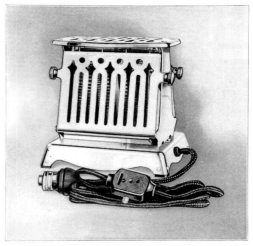

No. 202 L&H Electrics "Turnsit" Toaster

Height	...................7¼ in.	Volts	110-120
Width	...................7¼ in.	Watts	550
Depth	...................5¼ in.	Shipping Weight (3 Toasters)	...11 lbs.
Toasting Surface	...........4¾x5¾ in.	Code	...................Toastler

HEAVILY polished nickel finish. Heating element is braced on all sides with steel. It is nickel chromium ribbon handlaced and mica insulated. Separable attachment plug. Seven feet of silk heater cord with feed-through switch. The four fibre feet prevent marring table tops.

Showing Toaster Open

The "Turnsit" mechanism reverses the toast automatically each time the door is dropped. Extra large size of toasting surface—4¾x5¾"—permits toasting the largest slices of bread. A stop prevents shield from dropping on to and marring the table tops or scorching table linens. Handles prevent burning fingers. A draft check at the bottom of the door aids quicker, evener toasting. An extra large top provides suitable space for keeping toast warm. Each toaster wrapped in tissue and packed in a neat carton.

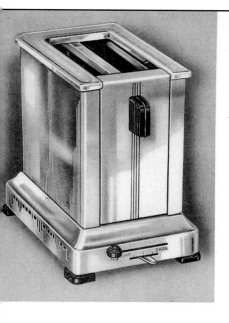

NEW BELL-SIGNAL TOASTER

Automatic Adjustable Heat Control for light, medium or dark toast.

Toasts both sides of two slices at a time, exactly the way you want them, and its gentle bell signals when toast is ready. At the same time the current is switched automatically from a toasting heat to a low serving heat which keeps toast warm until rack is manually released for serving. To make "Melba" toast leave in toaster for a few minutes after the bell rings. Diamond Luster Chromium Finish. Bakelite Handles and Feet.

No. E7122   Weight packed 5½ lbs.   Watts 800

Page from the 1937 "Reprinted" Universal Electrical Appliances catalog. Catalog with price list $75.00.

DOUBLE-QUICK OVEN TOASTER

An attractive toaster that makes crisp delicious oven toast at the table, two slices at a time. Needs no more space than the usual type of toaster. Ideal for families that require extra capacity. Toast rack tilts forward at the touch of a finger. Takes bread up to 4 x 4" inches. Finished in Gleaming Chromium with Black Bakelite Handles. Fibre Feet protect table.

No. E7722   Weight packed 4½ lbs.   Watts 800

Page from the 1930s Universal Commercial Electric Appliances catalog. Universal Electric, Landers, Frary & Clark. Showing the EC-70. "Oven is heated by five units. A dual switch that will omit two of these five units will make this appliance either a 2 or 4 slice toaster." Catalog price $75.00.

COMMERCIAL OVEN TYPE TOASTER
No. EC-70

DESIGNED on a new "ovenizing" principle this toaster makes toast better, faster and with far less expense than ordinary commercial toasters. The oven, entirely enclosing the bread, shields it from extraneous drafts and toasts it in a heat that is uniform at a great saving in electrical current. Every slice is toasted evenly, the toast never curls or dries. There is a marked saving in time as well as current consumption.

Adjustable and fully automatic, this toaster toasts to customers' taste with a minimum of time and attention. Signal light indicates whether current is on or off. Bread is placed on toast rack, oven door is closed, timing lever is pulled down and when bread is toasted, oven door automatically opens. Oven is heated by five units. A dual switch that will omit two of these five units makes of this appliance, either a two or four slice toaster, at desire of operator.

Toast may be timed from one-half to three minutes. Two hundred and forty slices of medium toast to the hour can easily be produced on standard voltage. Convenient release makes it possible to operate toaster independent of timer.

With a maximum capacity of 1500 watts, the new UNIVERSAL toaster is rated as a socket device, a feature that eliminates all expensive electrical installations.

For AC or DC.

WATTAGE
MAXIMUM
4 Slice .... 1500 watts
MINIMUM
2 Slice .... 945 watts
Standard Voltage 110 volt.

SPECIFICATIONS

Width	11½ in.
Depth	
Toast rack closed	11 in.
Toast rack open	13 in.
Height	12½ in.
Net Weight	19 lbs.
Shipping Weight	40 lbs.

LANDERS, FRARY & CLARK   **UNIVERSAL**   NEW BRITAIN, CONNECTICUT

Sunbeam TOASTWITCH

Completely Automatic. Makes Toast and Toasts Sandwiches Too.

Now truthfully, and for the first time, comes a toaster with which there is

No Waiting—It toasts two full slices, both sides at once. Makes toast faster than any other toaster ever made.

No Watching—Put the bread in, close the toaster. When done it shuts off the current, opens up itself, and raises up the front edge of the toast, so that it can be picked off comfortably.

No Turning—Toasts both sides of the two slices at once.

No Burning—Because when the toast is done it automatically shuts the current off and opens up. Keeps the toast warm until it is needed.

Adjustable for any kind of toast wanted —light, medium or full brown.

Toasts Sandwiches, Too

This new automatic toaster will also toast two full slice sandwiches, and the filling can't fall out, because they are toasted flat.

It also toasts halved rolls, crackers, etc., with the same speed and perfection.

This is really *the toaster that toasts anything well.*

The Sunbeam Toastwitch is truly a witch, because of the many things it does better than any other toaster ever made.

It cannot overheat, it cannot burn any one, it can never injure the finest table top, and it has ever cool handles, so that it can be moved anywhere at any time, and comfortably.

It is the easiest to clean of all automatic toasters. The heating element structure raises up, so that the reflector plate can be wiped off easily.

Beautiful, artistic, yet infinitely substantial and practical design. Chromium-plated throughout, richly polished, with handles of black bakelite. Will not rust or tarnish. Complete with full length cord and plug, packed in individual carton.

Catalog Number	Voltage	Wattage	Size of Carton	Number in Carton	Weight per Shipping Case	Number in Shipping Case	List Price
B5	110	660	12⅝x9¼x5½		6	50 lbs.	$17.50

— SUNBEAM APPLIANCES MAKE HAPPY HOMES —

[9]

Page from 1930 Sunbeam, The Best Electric Appliances Made, catalog No. 41-C. Showing the Sunbeam Toastwich and its uses. It also states it toasts crackers. This is really the toaster that toasts anything well. Special note: Catalog values are determined by condition, age, how much information, the number of toasters pictures shown, and the originally included price list. Catalog with price list $75.00.

Page from 1936 Electric Appliances by Manning-Bowman catalog. "Craftsman in Metal since 1864." Showing the Buffeteer toaster set. Each piece is decorated in the "Harmony" pattern. A number of toaster services have a matching pattern on all of the pieces. Catalog $75.00.

The Buffeteer Toaster Service

. . . is a boon to every hostess and a delight to every guest, for in addition to serving themselves, guests can actually make their own toast on the efficient Manning-Bowman two-slice Automatic Toaster, which is chromium finished. Bread may be toasted "light" or "dark" as preferred by simply moving the lever on the "Light-Dark" scale, in the base. The click of the control lever tells when the toast is done. A removable drawer in the base catches all crumbs.

The large and beautifully grained walnut serving tray is 25 by 15 inches. On it, besides the Automatic Toaster, are two double-compartment green pottery dishes for marmalades, jams, relishes, etc.; four walnut individual serving plates and a bread board. The unity of the design is especially appealing since each piece is decorated in the smart classic Harmony Pattern.

1080   Service Complete
Code "Algor"
Patented

WATTS 680   SHIPPING WEIGHT 16 LBS.
STANDARD PACKAGE 3

[26]

COLLECTOR BOOKS
Informing Today's Collector

DOLLS, FIGURES & TEDDY BEARS

2382	**Advertising Dolls**, Identification & Values, Robison & Sellers	$9.95
2079	**Barbie** Doll Fashions, Volume I, Eames	$24.95
3957	**Barbie** Exclusives, Rana	$18.95
4557	**Barbie**, The First 30 Years, Deutsch	$24.95
3310	**Black Dolls**, 1820–1991, Perkins	$17.95
3873	**Black Dolls**, Book II, Perkins	$17.95
3810	**Chatty Cathy** Dolls, Lewis	$15.95
4559	Collectible **Action Figures**, Manos	$17.95
1529	Collector's Encyclopedia of **Barbie** Dolls, DeWein	$19.95
4506	Collector's Guide to **Dolls in Uniform**, Bourgeois	$18.95
3727	Collector's Guide to **Ideal Dolls**, Izen	$18.95
3728	Collector's Guide to Miniature **Teddy Bears**, Powell	$17.95
3967	Collector's Guide to **Trolls**, Peterson	$19.95
3971	**Madame Alexander** Dolls Price Guide #20, Smith	$9.95
2186	**Modern Collector's** Dolls II, Smith	$17.95
2187	**Modern Collector's** Dolls III, Smith	$17.95
2188	**Modern Collector's** Dolls IV, Smith	$17.95
2189	**Modern Collector's** Dolls V, Smith	$17.95
3733	**Modern Collector's** Dolls, Sixth Series, Smith	$24.95
3991	**Modern Collector's** Dolls, Seventh Series, Smith	$24.95
3472	**Modern Collector's** Dolls Update, Smith	$9.95
3972	Patricia Smith's **Doll Values**, Antique to Modern, 11th Edition	$12.95
3826	Story of **Barbie**, Westenhouser	$19.95
1513	**Teddy Bears & Steiff** Animals, Mandel	$9.95
1817	**Teddy Bears & Steiff** Animals, 2nd Series, Mandel	$19.95
2084	**Teddy Bears, Annalee's & Steiff** Animals, 3rd Series, Mandel	$19.95
1808	Wonder of **Barbie**, Manos	$9.95
1430	World of **Barbie** Dolls, Manos	$9.95

TOYS, MARBLES & CHRISTMAS COLLECTIBLES

3427	**Advertising Character** Collectibles, Dotz	$17.95
2333	Antique & Collector's **Marbles**, 3rd Ed., Grist	$9.95
3827	Antique & Collector's **Toys**, 1870–1950, Longest	$24.95
3956	Baby Boomer **Games**, Identification & Value Guide, Polizzi	$24.95
1514	Character **Toys** & Collectibles, Longest	$19.95
1750	Character **Toys** & Collector's, 2nd Series, Longest	$19.95
3717	**Christmas** Collectibles, 2nd Edition, Whitmyer	$24.95
1752	**Christmas** Ornaments, Lights & Decorations, Johnson	$19.95
3874	Collectible Coca-Cola Toy **Trucks**, deCourtivron	$24.95
2338	Collector's Encyclopedia of **Disneyana**, Longest, Stern	$24.95
4566	Collector's Guide to **Tootsietoys, 2nd Ed** Richter	$19.95
3436	Grist's Big Book of **Marbles**	$19.95
3970	Grist's Machine-Made & Contemporary **Marbles**, 2nd Ed.	$9.95
3732	**Matchbox®** Toys, 1948 to 1993, Johnson	$18.95
3823	**Mego** Toys, An Illustrated Value Guide, Chrouch	15.95
1540	**Modern Toys** 1930–1980, Baker	$19.95
3888	**Motorcycle** Toys, Antique & Contemporary, Gentry/Downs	$18.95
4554	Schroeder's Collectible **Toys**, Antique to Modern Price Guide, 2nd Ed	$17.95
1886	Stern's Guide to **Disney** Collectibles	$14.95
2139	Stern's Guide to **Disney** Collectibles, 2nd Series	$14.95
3975	Stern's Guide to **Disney** Collectibles, 3rd Series	$18.95
2028	**Toys**, Antique & Collectible, Longest	$14.95
3974	**Zany Characters** of the Ad World, Lamphier	$16.95

JEWELRY, HATPINS, WATCHES & PURSES

1712	Antique & Collector's **Thimbles** & Accessories, Mathis	$19.95
1748	Antique **Purses**, Revised Second Ed., Holiner	$19.95
1278	Art Nouveau & Art Deco **Jewelry**, Baker	$9.95
3875	Collecting Antique **Stickpins**, Kerins	$16.95
3722	Collector's Ency. of **Compacts, Carryalls & Face Powder Boxes**, Mueller	$24.95
3992	Complete Price Guide to **Watches**, #15, Shugart	$21.95
1716	Fifty Years of Collectible **Fashion Jewelry**, 1925-1975, Baker	$19.95
1424	**Hatpins** & Hatpin Holders, Baker	$9.95
1181	100 Years of Collectible **Jewelry**, 1850-1950, Baker	$9.95
2348	20th Century Fashionable Plastic **Jewelry**, Baker	$19.95
3830	Vintage **Vanity Bags** & Purses, Gerson	$24.95

FURNITURE

1457	American **Oak** Furniture, McNerney	$9.95
3716	American **Oak** Furniture, Book II, McNerney	$12.95
1118	Antique **Oak** Furniture, Hill	$7.95
2132	Collector's Encyclopedia of **American** Furniture, Vol. I, Swedberg	$24.95
2271	Collector's Encyclopedia of **American** Furniture, Vol. II, Swedberg	$24.95
3720	Collector's Encyclopedia of **American** Furniture, Vol. III, Swedberg	$24.95
1437	Collector's Guide to **Country** Furniture, Raycraft	$9.95
3878	Collector's Guide to **Oak** Furniture, George	$12.95
1755	Furniture of the **Depression Era**, Swedberg	$19.95
3906	**Heywood-Wakefield** Modern Furniture, Rouland	$18.95
1965	**Pine** Furniture, Our American Heritage, McNerney	$14.95
1885	**Victorian** Furniture, Our American Heritage, McNerney	$9.95
3829	**Victorian** Furniture, Our American Heritage, Book II, McNerney	$9.95
3869	**Victorian** Furniture books, 2 volume set, McNerney	$19.90

INDIANS, GUNS, KNIVES, TOOLS, PRIMITIVES

1868	Antique **Tools**, Our American Heritage, McNerney	$9.95
2015	Archaic **Indian** Points & Knives, Edler	$14.95
1426	**Arrowheads** & Projectile Points, Hothem	$7.95
2279	**Indian** Artifacts of the Midwest, Hothem	$14.95
3885	**Indian** Artifacts of the Midwest, Book II, Hothem	$16.95
1964	**Indian** Axes & Related Stone Artifacts, Hothem	$14.95
2023	**Keen Kutter** Collectibles, Heuring	$14.95
3887	Modern **Guns**, Identification & Values, 10th Ed., Quertermous	$12.95
2164	**Primitives**, Our American Heritage, McNerney	$9.95
1759	**Primitives**, Our American Heritage, Series II, McNerney	$14.95
3325	Standard **Knife** Collector's Guide, 2nd Ed., Ritchie & Stewart	$12.95

PAPER COLLECTIBLES & BOOKS

1441	Collector's Guide to **Post Cards**, Wood	$9.95
2081	Guide to Collecting **Cookbooks**, Allen	$14.95
3969	Huxford's **Old Book** Value Guide, 7th Ed.	$19.95
3821	Huxford's **Paperback** Value Guide	$19.95
2080	Price Guide to **Cookbooks** & Recipe Leaflets, Dickinson	$9.95
3973	**Sheet Music** Reference & Price Guide, 2nd Ed., Pafik & Guiheen	$19.95

OTHER COLLECTIBLES

2280	Advertising **Playing Cards**, Grist	$16.95
2269	Antique **Brass & Copper** Collectibles, Gaston	$16.95
1880	Antique **Iron**, McNerney	$9.95
3872	Antique **Tins**, Dodge	$24.95
1714	**Black** Collectibles, Gibbs	$19.95
1128	**Bottle** Pricing Guide, 3rd Ed., Cleveland	$7.95
3959	**Cereal Box** Bonanza, The 1950's, Bruce	$19.95
3718	Collector's **Aluminum**, Grist	$16.95
4560	Collectible **Cats**, An Identification & Value Guide, Book II, Fyke	$19.95
1634	Collector's Ency. of Figural & Novelty **Salt & Pepper Shakers**, Davern	$19.95
2020	Collector's Ency. of Figural & Novelty **Salt & Pepper Shakers**, Vol. II, Davern	$19.95
2018	Collector's Encyclopedia of **Granite Ware**, Greguire	$24.95
3430	Collector's Encyclopedia of **Granite Ware**, Book II, Greguire	$24.95
3879	Collector's Guide to Antique **Radios**, 3rd Ed., Bunis	$18.95
1916	Collector's Guide to **Art Deco**, Gaston	$14.95
3880	Collector's Guide to **Cigarette Lighters**, Flanagan	$17.95
1537	Collector's Guide to **Country Baskets**, Raycraft	$9.95
3966	Collector's Guide to **Inkwells**, Identification & Values, Badders	$18.95
3881	Collector's Guide to **Novelty Radios**, Bunis/Breed	$18.95
3729	Collector's Guide to **Snow Domes**, Guarnaccia	$18.95
3730	Collector's Guide to **Transistor Radios**, Bunis	$15.95
2276	**Decoys**, Kangas	$24.95
1629	**Doorstops**, Identification & Values, Bertoia	$9.95
3968	**Fishing Lure** Collectibles, Murphy/Edmisten	$24.95
4568	**Flea Market Trader**, 10th Ed., Huxford	$12.95
3819	**General Store Collectibles**, Wilson	$24.95
2215	Goldstein's **Coca-Cola** Collectibles	$16.95
3884	Huxford's **Collector's Advertising**, 2nd Ed.	$24.95
2216	**Kitchen Antiques**, 1790–1940, McNerney	$14.95
1782	**1,000 Fruit Jars**, 5th Edition, Schroeder	$5.95
3321	Ornamental & Figural **Nutcrackers**, Rittenhouse	$16.95
2026	**Railroad** Collectibles, 4th Ed., Baker	$14.95
1632	**Salt & Pepper Shakers**, Guarnaccia	$9.95
1888	**Salt & Pepper Shakers** II, Identification & Value Guide, Book II, Guarnaccia	$14.95
2220	**Salt & Pepper Shakers** III, Guarnaccia	$14.95
3443	**Salt & Pepper Shakers** IV, Guarnaccia	$18.95
2096	**Silverplated Flatware**, Revised 4th Edition, Hagan	$14.95
1922	Standard **Old Bottle** Price Guide, Sellari	$14.95
3892	**Toy & Miniature Sewing Machines**, Thomas	$18.95
3828	Value Guide to **Advertising Memorabilia**, Summers	$18.95
3977	Value Guide to **Gas Station** Memorabilia	$24.95
3978	**Wanted to Buy**, 5th Edition	$9.95

This is only a partial listing of the books on collectibles that are available from Collector Books. All books are well illustrated and contain current values. Most of our books are available from your local bookseller, antique dealer, or public library. If you are unable to locate certain titles in your area, you may order by mail from COLLECTOR BOOKS, P.O. Box 3009, Paducah, KY 42002-3009. Customers with Visa or MasterCard may phone in orders from 7:00–5:00 CST, Monday–Friday, Toll Free 1-800-626-5420. Add $2.00 for postage for the first book ordered and $0.30 for each additional book. Include item number, title, and price when ordering. Allow 14 to 21 days for delivery.

Schroeder's
ANTIQUES
Price Guide

. . . is the #1 best-selling antiques & collectibles value guide on the market today, and here's why . . .

Schroeder's ANTIQUES Price Guide

OUR #1 BEST SELLER!

Identification & Values Of Over 50,000 Antiques & Collectibles

8½ x 11, 608 Pages, $12.95

• *More than 300 advisors, well-known dealers, and top-notch collectors work together with our editors to bring you accurate information regarding pricing and identification.*

• *More than 45,000 items in almost 500 categories are listed along with hundreds of sharp original photos that illustrate not only the rare and unusual, but the common, popular collectibles as well.*

• *Each large close-up shot shows important details clearly. Every subject is represented with histories and background information, a feature not found in any of our competitors' publications.*

• *Our editors keep abreast of newly developing trends, often adding several new categories a year as the need arises.*

If it merits the interest of today's collector, you'll find it in *Schroeder's*. And you can feel confident that the information we publish is up to date and accurate. Our advisors thoroughly check each category to spot inconsistencies, listings that may not be entirely reflective of market dealings, and lines too vague to be of merit. Only the best of the lot remains for publication.

Without doubt, you'll find
SCHROEDER'S ANTIQUES PRICE GUIDE
the only one to buy for
reliable information and values.

COLLECTOR BOOKS
A Division of Schroeder Publishing Co., Inc.